86 SMITH STREET

86 SMITH STREET

Joan Park

ISIS
LARGE PRINT
Oxford

Copyright © Joan Park, 2003

First published in Great Britain 2003
by ISIS Publishing Ltd.

Published in Large Print 2003 by ISIS Publishing Ltd.,
7 Centremcad, Osney Mead, Oxford OX2 0ES
by arrangement with the author

British Library Cataloguing in Publication Data
Park, Joan
    86 Smith Street. – Large print ed. –
    (Isis reminiscence series)
    1. Park, Joan – Childhood and youth
    2. Large type books
    3. Liverpool (England) – Biography
    4. Liverpool (England) – Social life and
    customs – 20th century
    I. Title   II. Eighty-six Smith Street
    942.7'53'083'092

ISBN 0–7531–9842–8 (hb)
ISBN 0–7531–9843–6 (pb)

Printed and bound by Antony Rowe, Chippenham

This book is written for my grandchildren,
Katherine, Rachel, Michael and Scott

Acknowledgements

I am indebted to the staff at Isis for their faith in an unknown writer of my vintage. I extend my gratitude to Jennifer Laurie, Kyle McKay and Irene Marcuson for their criticism and encouragement at various stages of the writing. Above all I wish to thank my daughter and my son for their unstinted assistance in providing me with the word-processing tools and enough of their expertise to enable my scribble to become presentable. Finally I thank my sister, Thelma, who filled in so many gaps in my memory.

Liverpool leans northward, a sore thumb separated from the fist of the Wirral peninsular by the five minute crossing on the Mersey ferry.

Via the Wirral it beckons to that Ancient British remnant in Wales who come seeking improvement through the university, the Playhouse and the Philarmonic. Dozens of pages of the Liverpool telephone directory are devoted to the Evans, the Hughes, the Llewis', the Owens, the Roberts and the Williams. Cast a glance at the names above the main department stores in the city centre and it is obvious that the Welsh are determined to stay. They are "in with the bricks".

It was the Welsh Nerys Hughes who was cast to play one of the Liver Birds in the television series. She played a character always defending her right to be heard and striving to move up the ladder of success yet sympathetic to her less fortunate friend, while her pretentious mother portrayed by Molly Sugden was a target for ridicule.

The chill wind which sweeps up from the Mersey making it less welcome to stand at a city bus stop than to face an Atlantic gale blows away all attemps at pretence. Perhaps it is the Welsh with their mainly Methodist background who have given to Liverpool an openness, an honesty and an intolerance of "side".

Undeterrred by the longer sail across the Irish sea at the estuary of the Mersey the Irish have been landing regularly since the potato famine left the first of them jobless. Together with their paltry baggage, they carry that unquenchable zest for life which finds humour in adversity. How else could Liverpool have produced an Arthur Askey, a Jimmy Tarbuck, a Ken Dodd and a Tom O'Connor, all in the wake of a second world war?

The humour of the Murphys and the Kellys dominates the "cop" every Saturday at Anfield urging "the Pool" to victory over Everton and disputing each verdict of the referee. Similarly the police suffer from the quips of the "Del Boys" when requiring them to pack up their suitcases and move on. The Canavans and the O'Connors have so influenced the Liverpool way of life that any figure of authority is bait for lampooning, while the law exists only to stretch efforts to flout it.

Every second man in Liverpool is a Paddy's lawyer, arguing wrong is right. All are born with the gift of the gab. Modesty and reticence are foreign notions to young "scousers". Inspired by the fame of Cilla Black and the Beatles, every child sees himself as a future star of either football field or stage.

From Lancashire, east of Liverpool, tamer neighbours cross the city boundary to visit and even work, but scurry home each night thankful to be leaving Liverpool behind. The resident population, in its turn, escapes north to the Lake District for day and weekend trips, only to bewail the absence of fish and chip shops which could be found in abundance and closer at hand in Blackpool.

New York has its Statue of Liberty to welcome immigrants; Liverpool has its Liver Birds perched on the Waterfront at the Pier Head. The Statue of Liberty was inspired by the spirit of the French Revolution, an historic event; the Liver Bird, a hybrid resembling no existing bird, like the Phoenix is rooted in myth. Along with New York, Liverpool has always accepted the poor and the oppressed; East Europeans, Chinese and West Indians. There was a Chinese laundry two blocks away from where I lived in Smith Street in the 1930s and our neighbours were the Lapins and Baraslovskis.

It is this mix of nationalities which gives Liverpool its inventive, all-embracing language by which bus drivers and shopkeepers address every adult as "luv" or "luvvie"; where smokers light a "ciggie"; where children express their need to go to the "lavvie" and every comment is embellished with "Ye know". It is odd that such a loquacious group of citizens should choose to use such an incomprehensible accent. Outsiders who fail to emulate it have never mastered the knack of blocking the nose, holding the mouth open when in repose but closing it and clenching the teeth tightly when actually speaking. It is of some significance that the actor who came nearest to this, in playing Alf Garnett's son-in-law in the television series *Till Death Us Do Part*, was Anthony Booth, the father-in-law of Prime Minister Tony Blair.

A short walk from Liverpool's Chinatown, and in the same street as one another, stand the two cathedrals, one for the "Proddydogs" and the other known affectionately to all as "Paddy's Umbrella". Their two bishops worked tirelessly together through the 1960s and 1970s in an area infamous for the riots against the Thatcher government. Symbolically this area is named Hope Street. Hope epitomises the conglomerate of Liverpool. Little remains of the once thriving port or of the affluence produced by the slave trade, but every true Liver Bird would refuse to think of Liverpool as a deprived area or a dead city. Instead he is certain it will rise from the ashes.

A stubborn, arrogant lot, Liverpudlians are proud of their city with its cosmopolitan mix of cultures. They are proud to be more akin to the people north of the border than those south of the Midlands. To be a Liverpudlian is to fiercely protect your own corner while grudgingly admitting the right of your opponent to defend his. It is lending a hand or a quid to your neighbour while denying that you are ever in need. Above all it is an inability to admit that your dreams are beyond your reach.

Joan Park

1927

It is a winter morning. I am sitting on a stool beside a glowing fire in a newly black-leaded grate and my mother is holding a long black toasting fork to the bottom bars of the grate. It holds a slice of pilot loaf. When it is brown, she will butter it for me and slice it into fingers and I will dip the "soldiers" into my boiled egg. In the kitchen there is just my mother and me, for my big sister has left for school in her navy reefer coat and velour hat. She is five and a half and I am two and a half years old.

My mother wears a large, sleeveless, wrap-around overall hiding most of the dress underneath and, covering her auburn hair, she wears a dust-cap.

She sings as she moves the things from the top of the dresser, dusting them as each in turn is laid on the gate-legged table that stands opposite the fire-place: "She is the lily of Laguna, she is my lily and my rose." There is a smell that is a mixture of Mansion polish, the newly toasted bread, the glass of hot milk and the polished apples in the dish on the dresser.

I hear Granddad's footsteps, the "dot and carry one" of his tread, as he mounts the half-dozen stairs that lead up to the kitchen from the shop beyond where he works as a shoe-repairer.

"Keep an eye on the counter, Nan, I won't be a tick," and hurriedly he limps through to the back-kitchen door and out to the lavatory in the yard.

As he returns, Mother says, "Are you on your own in the shop, Dad? I thought Jack Fletcher was coming in today to do the finishing."

"He's only popped out for a bit to pick up a newspaper."

"Pick up racing tips, you mean!"

Granddad goes, "dot and carry one," back into the shop and minutes later Nursie appears for her usual mid-morning chat. Her real name is Nurse McKinlay and she is my mother's best friend.

"Your Dad's leg seems a bit worse than usual today, Nan. It's time he saw a doctor."

"You try telling him that. I've been at him for weeks."

"I'll see the doctor later on today. He's attending one of my cases. I'll mention it. Must rush now. I promised Ernie I'ld take over the shop while he gets to the bank."

"How is business these days?"

"We can't grumble, not as bad as some. The sweet shop has had to close down. Word is they've gone bankrupt."

"That doesn't surprise me. I wouldn't buy sweets from them. All those open trays of sweets in the window for the rats to crawl over!"

"How will you manage if your Dad has to take to his bed?"

"I'll manage. I keep Dad's books now. There's Mr Mann working full time and I daresay Jack Fletcher would be glad of the extra money if I gave him a couple of extra days a week. I wouldn't trust him with the counter. Chances are he'd help himself to the till.

Spring 1927

Today I am sitting on the bottom stair at the corner of the kitchen. The doctor has just gone upstairs to put a dressing on Granddad's sore leg. On the days that the doctor doesn't come a nurse comes. They both carry black, leather bags like Nursie's. Mummy has given me an old handbag so that I can play at being a district nurse.

When the doctor goes away I will be able to go back upstairs and sit on Granddad's bed. I have been able to climb upstairs for some time now and nobody minds so long as I come down one step at a time on my bottom.

Summer 1927

It is a Wednesday afternoon and early closing day in my Granddad's boot-repairer's. On my mother's bed lies my favourite dress. It is pink organdie with white daisies embroidered round the hem. Mummy is sitting at her dressing table putting Pond's Vanishing Cream on her face.

"Can I have some on my face so I can smell like you?"

My mother laughs and puts a little smear on my nose and hugs me.

"You can put your dress on, now." she says, "We'll need to hurry. We don't want to be late for the hospital."

We walk to Stanley Road hospital. Granddad is sitting up in a bed near the open doors that lead into the ground-floor ward. On his bed is a bright scarlet blanket. My mother bends down and kisses him and for a brief moment I am allowed to climb up on the red blanket for him to hold me in his arms. He brushes his sandy-grey moustache against my cheek and I would like to climb into that cosy bed beside him.

"Go and say hello to Mr. Higgins." Granddad bids me and I walk round to Dan Higgins who has had the bed next to Granddad in all the months we have visited the hospital.

"How are things in the shop, Nan?"

"Much as usual, Dad. I don't know what we would do without Mann. He works hard. Wish I could say the same for Jack Fletcher. He spends more time studying form in the racing papers than he does working. I'll be giving him a piece of my mind one of these days."

"Now, now, Nan, he's not such a bad stick. Did that traveller turn up with the boot-polish and the insoles as he promised?"

"He did. His bill came in yesterday. And the rates are due next week. I'm having to cut down on the credit you extend to half your customers, Dad. We need the cash."

"Which customers do you have in mind?"

"Those out-of-work lay-abouts; that Roberts family for a start. She had the cheek to bring in his boots again and he won't be getting them back until he's paid for the last repairs."

"You're hard, Nan. There's more of your mother in you than I thought. That man's got a wife and young uns. How can he go out and look for work without his boots?"

"Well, if I'm hard, it's only because you're too soft. How do you expect to make the shop pay if you work for nothing?"

"We get by. Most of the time it gives us a living. I don't ask for more. I couldn't sleep in my bed at nights thinking of that man without his boots."

We hurry home so as to be there before Thelma comes home from school. My sister's full name is Thelma Madeline Lowe because my mother read a book called Thelma. Auntie Muriel, that is Daddy's sister, wanted her name to be Magdalen but Mother said that was a bad woman in the Bible. Thelma has long ringlets. Each night my mother winds strips of rag round the strands of hair and next morning when she takes the rags out the ringlets are there.

I have only one name and that is Joan because my mother says that is the name of many of her favourite film stars. My Daddy's favourite film star is Norma Shearer and I think Norma is a prettier name than Joan. If I could choose my own name it would be Beryl. I, too, would like to have ringlets but my hair is cut short and I have a fringe. My mother hates her own name which is Annie Maria, so everyone calls her Nan. My Daddy is called Gerald Frank Arthur and his shipmates call him Gerry. Mother says, "Gerry is common" and she calls him Gerald.

Daddy is usually away at sea. He is a bedroom steward on passenger ships that sail to China and Japan. He comes home after a three-month voyage and he always brings lots of presents. He brought the cane chairs and the grass mats that are in the bedrooms. If you slit open bits of the grass with your nails you can take out the hardened sap and it tastes quite good. Thelma and I have silk kimonos that we wear as summer dressing gowns and Daddy brings lengths of tussore for Cousin Nan to make us blouses and dresses. Granddad's present is sometimes a Chinese puzzle, made up of pieces of wood which all fit together to make a barrel. We have a wooden mummy which opens up to reveal a second mummy inside her and so on until there are five or six mummies, each a little smaller than the one that held it.

On the dressing table in Mummy and Daddy's bedroom there's a linen duchesse set, embroidered with pagodas and rickshaws and tiny people. Mummy has a powder compact and a cigarette case which are black with little scenes of snow-topped Mount Fuji worked in silver and gold and mother-of-pearl.

Mummy has two gold bracelets. One is called a slave bracelet and she shows us the teeth marks we made as babies when we cut our teeth on it. The other bracelet is made up of half-sovereigns, all linked together which Daddy gave her when she was twenty-one.

Autumn 1927

Today, because my Daddy is home, Mummy is wearing her best dress. It is saxe-blue and has short, loose sleeves which are slit open to reveal the flame lining. My Daddy strokes her arm and kisses it. I take her other arm and kiss it and say, "She's my Mummy."

They both laugh and Daddy says, "She's my Mummy. I knew her first."

"She's not your Mummy." I insist, "She's my Mummy." and because the game goes on too long I end up crying so that Mummy will have to take me on her knee.

I know my Daddy sent me to my Mummy from the Antena and I know that he sent Thelma from the Aeneas (We pronounce it "A-knee-ass") because Mummy says so, and although I'm grateful for that, I am really Mummy's little girl.

I do like my Daddy being at home because we all go for days out together and there's lots of treats like half-penny ice-cream cornets. I like the smell of his pipe tobacco in the house.

August 1928

It is my fourth birthday and for the first time, ever, I am the reason for a children's birthday party. I am dressed in my best frock. I eat the sandwiches and cakes and jellies and see my mother carrying the big, white, iced birthday cake into the back-kitchen.

Presently the guests leave, carrying away their slices of cake in paper serviettes. One big wedge of cake sits on the dresser. I regard this with approval. It is obvious that this is the biggest piece of all, and it is to be mine because it is my birthday.

"I'm just popping in to Nurse McKinlays," says my mother. "I'm taking her this piece of cake."

With this she wraps up my piece of cake. The party is over. The cake has disappeared and I am left wondering why my mother has not realised that I have not tasted a single mouthful of my first and only iced birthday cake.

Spring 1929

Thelma and I are in the back yard. The privets are in leaf. The clumps of last year's Golden Rod and Michaelmas Daisies in the narrow strip of soil at the bottom of the yard attract their usual host of flies. In the side border, below the privet, a few primulas struggle to bloom, their leaves a dusty green. There is a single Tiger Lily. It is a creeper-covered, walled yard. Our neighbours on one side are the Lapins: Maurice and Hymie, who are brothers, and Maurice's wife, whom I call Mrs Lapin. They are money-lenders. I think they are rich and wonder why is it that Granddad is always lending money but is not rich?

The Lapins must have lots of money. I know this must be so because Mrs. Lapin has just returned from a visit to the United States of America. She brought back some coloured comic papers and passed them in to us. Thelma and I got a brief glance at them before Mother chucked them in the bin.

"Pure rubbish! What could you learn from them except American slang? No, thank you. They're for people who can't read."

On the other side of the yard live the Baraslovskis. Mona and Norman and Cyril sometimes pop their heads over the wall. They all have tight curly hair and rosy cheeks. I wish I had curly hair and rosy cheeks.

"Mummy, how could I get curly hair?"

"Eating up the crusts on your bread and butter."

"Is that how Mona and Norman and Cyril got their curly hair?"

"God knows! From the smells that come from next door I don't think they eat much that hasn't been cooked in oil."

"Does that give them curly hair and rosy cheeks?"

"I doubt it. Good beef dripping never did anyone any harm."

"Could the oil make them die?"

"Of course not. I'm not suggesting it's poison."

"I wouldn't want them to die. I'm going to marry Cyril when I grow up."

Mother adjusts the sheets, blowing on the line and has a brief word with Mrs. Baraslovski who is collecting her washing.

"Mr. Payne not home from hospital yet, Mrs. Lowe?"

"We're expecting him home to-day. I've just this minute finished making the house tidy and I'm about to cook the dinner."

"It's been a long time, Mrs. Lowe, with you managing the shop and the house and the children."

"I'm not saying I won't be glad to have my dad home. Two years it is since he first took ill."

"Really! Is it that long? Lonely for you with your husband away most of the time. When is he due home?"

"Next month."

"You need a break."

"If it turns out he has to work by the ship in Glasgow and my dad can manage on his own, I'll maybe go up to Glasgow for a few days with the children."

Mother returns to the back kitchen.

"When will Granddad get here?"

"Not long now, you'll hear the taxi arrive."

"Can we go to the shop door and watch for it coming?"

"It's too soon. Just play in the yard while I'm busy."

"We're busy too. We're making a dinner for Granddad. Look."

I hold out a tiny tin plate, a remnant from some former dolls' tea-set. On it are torn up privet leaves.

Mother looks and says, "Is that the cabbage? I thought you didn't like cabbage."

"You know I hate it. I hate cabbage and sprouts and curlygreen. I only like peas. Is it peas today? What's for dinner? What's for pudding?"

"Wait and see. It's a surprise. There won't be any dinner if I don't get the meat in the oven."

We pick more privet leaves and tear them up into tiny pieces. It is a very long morning. Suddenly I look up and through the kitchen window I see Granddad, sitting in his cushioned, cane club chair. I'm momentarily devastated because I missed seeing the taxi but I'm so excited that Granddad is home again that the disappointment recedes as I race inside.

After dinner I am sitting on Granddad's knee. His crutches lean against the side of his chair and he is reading a story to me. It tells of Blackie, a baby rat, and how his Mummy and Daddy find an egg and they can't think how to get it home so baby Blackie lies down on his back, puts his legs up to hold the egg on his tummy, and gets pushed along like a wheelbarrow.

"Is it a true story?" I ask.

"Well, yes. It's true that rats carry away eggs."

"Let's have the next story."

Granddad turns the page.

"Once upon a time . . ." I say, because I recognise the familiar words.

"she can read, Nan."

"No, she can't. She just knows what some words look like on the page."

"You should let her start school."

"Good God! Dad, she's only four. There's plenty of time. We'd have to find another lot of school fees for Spellow Lane."

"We can manage that. Talk to the Sharps. Perhaps they'll consider a reduction in fees for the second child."

"I'll talk to Nurse McKinlay some time."

★ ★ ★

Hardly a day passes that Nurse McKinlay or Nursie, as we call her, doesn't drop in for a cup of tea and a chat. This usually lasts an hour. She is my mother's best friend and she is the local midwife. When she is not on her rounds or talking to my mother she helps her brother, Ernie Sharp, serve in his grocer's shop, a few doors away. Ernie delivers our weekly order but sometimes Thelma or I are sent for some item.

"Half a pound of butter, please."

I can just reach the polished dark wood counter to see him taking a lump of butter from the barrel-shaped tower that stands on the back shelf behind him. He works it between two long wooden platters, slapping it from one to the other for a while, before finally patting it into a rough square, ridged where the platters have left their imprint.

"I hear you are going to school soon."

"I've already been."

"Well, I never! And when was that?"

"I went to the Christmas party in Thelma's class."

"Were there a lot of good things to eat?"

"Just biscuits and sweets. Each of us had to sing a song or say a poem."

"Did you sing a song?"

"I said a poem. It was all about Christmas."

I don't tell Ernie that when I had reached the line, "The tables piled high with puddings and pies," I had raised my arms in the appropriate action, only to hear my sister's loud whisper of "Joan, you're showing your knickers."

How dare she interrupt my party piece? I was indignant,

"They're cleaner than yours, anyway."

I suppose I then went on to finish the poem because I sat down to much applause and amusement from my audience, in praise, I thought, of my performance.

I don't tell Ernie this story because Mummy says knickers are not things to talk about.

It is Monday and it is washing day. There are steep steps leading down to the cellar where Mummy does the washing. I have been taken down to the stone-floored cellar to see the wooden dolly-tub, the wash-board, the wringer, a big iron contraption with wooden rollers, sometimes called the mangle, and the huge copper boiler heated by the gas flames beneath it.

On the far side, against a wall, is a stack of coal. Above the coal is a grating. This is lifted at pavement level when the horse-drawn coal cart stops outside our boot-repairing shop at 86 Smith Street. The men climb down from the cart, wearing sacks over their heads and shoulders. They stand with their backs against the open cart, the better to heave onto them the hundredweight sacks which are then emptied into the coal-hole. My sister Thelma and I watch this from one of the big windows in the upstairs sitting room which looks out on to the busy street and the tram sheds opposite. Even if we are not at the window we know when the coal is being delivered because we hear it rumbling down into the cellar. It makes a lot of dust so the walls of the cellar have to be white-washed several times a year. On

13

days when I look particularly grubby, Mummy says, "You look as if you'd spent the day down the coal-hole.'

I am not allowed to go down the cellar steps on my own in case I fall. The smell that seeps up from the cellar does not tempt me into disobedience. It is a mixture of caustic soda and the bits of reesty fat which have been saved over the weeks and months. Mummy boils these together to make her own soap; a horrid, sickly yellow substance not in the least resembling the soap we use in the bathroom which may be Lifebuoy Toilet, Wrights Coal Tar, or the more luxurious Amami or Pears, which everybody knows makes you beautiful.

Thelma and I take it in turns to ask for the soap wrapper to put into a dressing-table drawer to perfume our handkerchiefs. We cover our faces with soap lather, much as Granddad does when he is shaving, knowing that one day we too will look like the golden-haired child featured in the newspaper advertisements. There I also see advertisements for Rinso and Restu, soap powders which my mother considers an extravagance although she relents sufficiently to buy Lux soap flakes for the handwashing of best clothes. The Lux packet stands on the back-kitchen windowsill above the sink. We do not use it for washing dishes.

For that there is a small metal mesh container holding all the scraps of old soap. It has a handle attached so that it can be shaken in the hot water to make suds.

Because it is washday I play in Granddad's workshop. He gives me chips of leather, a small hammer, a rasp, a few tacks and some used sandpaper.

14

He clears a space on one of the three workbenches for me and carries on with his own work further up the bench where he stands resting against rather than sitting on the stool behind him. The boot that Granddad is repairing fits over the heavy iron last. The pincers grab the old sole and rip it away complete with the nails that held it fast. The rough rectangle of new leather is slapped on the boot and a few nails hammered in to hold it in place. A sharp knife trims the piece of leather to the shape of the sole, the leather parings bouncing off the bench and floor.

Granddad takes a handful of tacks, throws back his head and at the same time flings the tacks into his open mouth from which he spits them singly as they are hammered evenly round the edge of the sole. A rasp and sandpaper complete the trimming. The heel is repaired in much the same way. Protectors, little, kidney-shaped, metal studs are applied to take the brunt of the wear and tear or, in some cases, these are replaced by rubber tips held in position by the rubber solution which smells so strongly that my eyes water and the tang of new leather is almost obliterated. The repaired boot is thrown into the pile to await its turn at the finishing machine which all this time is whirring away at the front window.

Jack Fletcher stands at the wheel, turning a shoe so that each part of the repair will get its black, resin finish to make it look like new. The spots of heel-ball spatter on to the light brown, overall coats of the men in the shop, cling to their faces and hair and to my pinafore.

There is a partition, the length of the workshop, separating the customer entrance from the workmen. From time to time I hear the bell that rings as the shop door is opened and someone approaches the counter. It is usually Granddad who leaves his work to deal with the customer and I hear him ring up the purchase on the wooden till that stands at the foot of the five wooden stairs that lead into the kitchen.

To the right of the finisher is a door which leads out of the workshop to the main door on to Smith Street. In the pane of glass in the top half of the door is a poster of a man holding a shoe. He is saying, "Phillips' heels are best." The man has a moustache, just like Granddad's and for a long time I am sure it is a picture of my Granddad. He is the only shoe-maker I know; the only shoemaker in my very small world.

Thelma comes home from school and, promptly, at one o'clock, the shop is closed. Granddad, Jack Fletcher and Mr Mann walk up the stairs and go through the kitchen to use the outside lavatory that stands in the back yard. They wash their hands at the back-kitchen sink and come through to sit with us at the gate-legged table, set for midday dinner.

On washday it is always Scouse. Scouse is made from the left-over meat of the Sunday roast, together with carrots, onions and potatoes all cooked in a pan on top of the gas stove. I think it is not nearly as tasty as Hotpot, cooked in an earthenware dish in the coal oven, next to the fire which burns winter and summer.

"I don't like scouse," I say, as we begin to eat, "there's not enough gravy."

"I know some children who'd be glad to eat it," snaps my mother, "If you want to get a pudding, you'll clear your plate."

Pudding, too, is a disappointment. On a washday it has to be something easy. While I do not mind rice pudding if it is creamy from long, slow cooking in the oven, I have to force myself to swallow the lumps in sago and tapioca puddings. Hot, stewed rhubarb is even worse when the pouring custard curdles as it reaches the juice. My favourite puddings, which I can never expect on a washday are the ones Mummy makes in the steamer. It hisses away all morning making plum or apple suet pudding and, on very special occasions, jam sponge which we have with white sauce.

"Good day for getting the clothes dry," Granddad observes, looking out of the window above the dresser into the back yard where the sheets, pillowcases, towels and tablecloths fill the available line space.

"I'll get them in, now, if that's all right with you, Dad. There's another load down in the cellar ready to be hung out. Can you keep an eye on Joan for the few minutes you've got before you open the shop? Time you were getting ready for school, Thelma."

"Take your time, We'll have a story book."

"Bobby Bear?" I ask.

"Bobby Bear it is," says Granddad as he moves to his easy chair, and I collect the book and climb up on his knee.

The little window on one side of our kitchen looks out on to the shop. Below the window is a cretonne-covered sofa. The black-leaded grate with its side oven and hob holding two iron kettles fills up most of the width of the kitchen on one wall. On the opposite wall is the gate-legged table with its wooden chairs. At the end of this wall are the stairs which lead to the bathroom, Granddad's bedroom and the upstairs sitting room. Beyond them and up another flight of stairs are the other bedrooms. On the remaining wall of the kitchen is the larger window that looks out on to our back yard. Below this window sits the kitchen dresser with its plain wooden top which frequently gets scrubbed.

By climbing up on Granddad's cushioned chair, I can reach the top of the dresser. I can lick a caramel and then put it back inside its paper or I can take a bite out of a rosy apple and carefully turn it round so that, looking at the dish, no-one can see it has had a bite taken out of it.

"Believe it or not," says my mother, "there's a two-legged mouse in this house that takes bites out of the apples when I'm not looking."

"That's fine," I think, "she doesn't guess it's me." And, though I have never heard of a two-legged mouse, in my mind I picture one standing on its two hind legs and postpone my questions about it until another day.

At the back of the dresser stand Granddad's emulsion and a bottle of Owbridge's cough mixture. When my mother gives me cough mixture she puts a spoonful in a drop of warm water and stirs it to make a delicious brown drink. I've tasted Granddad's emulsion but I don't like it. There's also a jar of malt. Daily, in winter, Thelma and I are each given a teaspoonful of malt. This is to build us up and keep us free of colds. It tastes like melted toffee. Next to the malt is the syrup of figs. We have to take this every Friday night to avoid constipation. I hate syrup of figs so I've found a way of keeping it in my mouth until I can spit it out somewhere when Mother is not looking. The trouble is you have to hold the taste longer than if you swallowed it.

The reason I climb up on Granddad's chair is to have a little rummage in Granddad's drawer. All the other dresser drawers have uninteresting things like tablecloths and serviettes and cutlery. Compared with these, Granddad's drawer is a glorious collection of odds and ends.

"Bring me a tin opener," Mother shouts from the back kitchen.

"Where is it?" we shout back.

"Look in Granddad's drawer."

Similarly, that is where we would look for a drawing pin or a nutcracker, a bottle of aspirins or some cough lozenges. Today I find no cough lozenges to lick but I do find a little flat tin containing sweets of a kind. These are Granddad's Tiz tablets. One lick tells me they do not have a nice taste. It surprises me the next time Granddad is soaking his corns in a bowl beside the fire to see him open this tin and drop a Tiz tablet into the water. No wonder they do not taste good. Perhaps if I had swallowed one I would have died and at my funeral they would have sung, "There's a friend for little children above the bright blue sky. And all who follow Jesus will go there by and by."

It is my favourite hymn.

★ ★ ★

I am sitting at a desk in Miss Grasby's classroom. On either side of me are Marguerite Sawberg and Doreen Leece who are to be my school friends for the next five years. We look at a chart on the wall and, following the letters which the teacher indicates with a wooden pointer, we repeatedly sing the alphabet. Sometimes we copy out the letters on to slates with squeaky slate pencils. At the end of the lesson we rub our slates clean with our hands a then copy numbers.

"Get out your reading books," and we shuffle out our books from the shelves below the sloping, wooden desk tops, supported by iron frames, screwed to the floor, as are also the benches we sit on.

"Now, children, look at the words on page three and keep looking while I read them to you."

She begins to read, "So, No, Go," a list of about six words, "Now each of you in turn will come out to my desk when I call your name and I will see if you can read them to me."

My turn comes and, beside the teacher's desk, I look her confidently in the eye and recite the memorised list of words.

She raps the desk with her ruler, saying loudly, "No, you must look at the words in the book so that I know you can read them."

I do as bidden, thinking meanwhile that I do not understand this reading business. Of course I can read the words. Has she not just told us what they were?

It is afternoon, now, and we are tearing strips from sample sheets of wallpaper and winding them round a knitting needle to make beads which we thread into necklaces.

It is a lovely, sunny day and my mother is coming to meet us from school to take us to New Brighton. We take the tram down to the Pier Head and race down the covered passage leading to the landing stage, our voices and footsteps echoing as we run. We are just in time to catch the ferry boat. I hug the side of the boat as the men on the landing stage loosen the ropes that are secured round the capstans and throw them to the crew on board. Sometimes the ropes trail through the water and the seamen, in their peaked caps and navy-blue jerseys, haul them aboard, dripping and making pools on the deck.

Thelma and I dodge the puddles, race up the steep, metal stairs and run to where Mother has found a seat on the upper deck. We eat some of the egg sandwiches and drink cold milk which she has brought from home.

"Any bread for the seagulls?" we ask and, with the stale crusts, we kneel on the wooden, slatted benches and lean over the rails as the gulls sweep down.

"Can we run round and play?"

"Just be careful. We don't want any more skinned knees."

We play Hide and Seek.

The boat calls at Seacombe and we watch as the gangways are lowered for some people to go ashore and others to board. Sometimes we get off the boat at Seacombe and walk along the promenade to New

Brighton. This takes nearly an hour. I would rather have that time to play at New Brighton.

Today we sail all the way because Mother has a contract. This is a ticket which allows her to travel at a cheap rate on the Mersey ferries all summer long. The child's ferry ticket costs twopence, fed into a slot machine on board.

We urge Mother to stand near the gangway as the boat nears its final destination. We want to be first to get ashore.

"Penny for the diver!" a voice shouts through a megaphone from the pier and all eyes turn to the figure that dives from the pier into the murky depths of the Mersey. We all clap as he surfaces and climbs back on to the pier for his next performance.

As we run the length of the pier we see the black water lapping below the slits in the planks and realise it is high tide. No sand! Oh, the dreadful disappointment!

"The tide's on the turn," Mother consoles us, "Besides, we can go to Reece's." So, the first stop is Reece's cafe on the promenade. We don't go into the cafe as there is an outside service counter where we buy fresh buns and cold milk.

"There's a bit of sand," we shout, as we cross the promenade from the cafe.

"That's dirty sand," Mother says, "The tide hardly ever comes up far enough to wash it. It just harbours fleas. We'll go to the rock pools."

The red sandstone rocks have already dried in the sun and we jump from boulder to boulder, stopping to search the pools for shells and crabs. Mother finds a smooth rock to sit on. Off come the shoes and socks and the gingham dresses get tucked into the knickers as we set about one of our favourite games. This involves take a smooth pebble to break off lumps of sandstone and mash it down to a pulp. We mould it, like plasticine, to make little cakes and bun loaves like Auntie Polly bakes for us at Christmas. Our bakery products are laid out on a rock and they dry hard in the sun.

Soon, we move to a smooth stretch of clean sand, waiting to be dug. We make sand-pies and, with Mother's help, build a castle. Digging round it to make a moat we strike water. We race to and fro, between the beach and the waves, filling our small buckets and emptying them into the moat, except the level of water in the moat never seems to rise.

When we relinquish the struggle to flood the moat, Thelma, who is going to have a bakery when she grows up, digs a hole in the wet sand, deep enough to reach the water lurking below, plunges in her hands up to her elbows and brings out a handful of sloppy sand. This she throws from hand to hand until she has fashioned a doughnut which she flops on to a stretch of smooth sand. She hands me the bucket and says, "Race up to the steps and bring me some of the sugary sand to sprinkle on the doughnuts."

Our play continues until the heat goes out of the sun when we polish off the rest of the egg sandwiches and bananas and have a final paddle in the waves to dislodge the sand from between our toes. Our feet sink in the sugary sand we have to tramp through to reach the steps that lead up to the promenade. We carry buckets of water so that once again we can get rid of the sand.

When we reach home there is yet another treat in store.

"How about fish and chips?" Mother asks and then, as she hands us the money and the tureen, "Remember, no salt and vinegar and make sure you get the freshest batch of chips. We don't want the end of the last lot that have lain there for ten minutes."

There is a queue all round the walls of the chip shop a few doors down in Smith Street. We stand amid the mixed smells of fish, hot fat and vinegar and the sounds of the fat sizzling and the splash and hiss as the chips are plunged into the trough of hot fat. When we reach the corner of the counter we catch a glimpse of the fish, newly battered, waiting to be thrown into the fat. I cannot reach the high counter but there is a ledge a little above floor level on which I manage to balance in order to catch a better view of the sheets of newspaper into which are scooped the portions of chips, the salt and vinegar applied and banged down again on the counter between each purchase.

"Two fish and sixpennyworth of chips," we say and to our relief we see the basket of fresh chips removed from the fat, shaken and drained of fat and tossed into the metal trough from which they are served.

"No salt and vinegar, thank you," we say as ours are put into the tureen.

Granddad has a whole battered fish while Mother breaks a bit off hers to give us a taste as we share the chips.

24

I go to bed with the salty smells of the Mersey in my nostrils and the echoes of "Penny for the diver!" singing in my ears.

I am dressed in my best coat and hat that I wear for Sunday School. The coat is new and Cousin Nan made it. It is in the newest Princess Elizabeth style with a fitted waist and full skirt.

"Well, now, don't you look the smart ones!" This from the grey-haired, uniformed commissionaire who stands at the revolving doors of the shipping office in India Buildings where we go, once a month, to collect the "allotment," the part of my father's wages which mother receives. It is thirty shillings and it doesn't always last the month but we borrow from Granddad. When Daddy comes home every three months from his sea trips he has a lot of money in tips and with that we buy new hats and shoes.

The commissionaire guides us through the revolving doors and we are allowed to go round in them several times before emerging into the shipping office with its grilled counters. The staff are very friendly for they know us well and they, too, comment on our new coats.

From the shipping office we walk round to Coopers in Church Street. Coopers is my favourite shop. It is possible to spend ages there for there is much to look at and smell and taste. It starts in the doorway because the very first stand is selling the newly ground coffee, the aroma of which follows us all through the shop. We buy a quarter of a pound of ground coffee and when my mother makes it she will sprinkle some on to the top of a pan of milk, letting it slowly simmer for a long while before she strains it into a jug. We only have it rarely. At the biscuit counter we may buy half a pound of currant creams or even a tin of Motoring biscuits if we have reason to make it a special occasion.

I like the days that my mother leaves Thelma and me in Coopers while she does other shopping. Of course, Thelma dictates the rate of our progress. We have sixpence each to spend. I choose the liquorice Pontefract cakes because you get a lot for your money. The assistant weighs them out and they are presented in a delightful paper dorothy bag, drawn together by coloured cord. Thelma has a more refined taste. She makes her selection from the cake decorations; a tiny jar of rose or violet sugar petals or silver balls. She doesn't eat these and so, while I am tucking in to the Pontefract cakes, she has us linger at the cheese counter in order to sample tiny squares of cheese on scraps of water biscuit or cream cracker.

We move on to the huge hot plate where staff in tall chef hats and white aprons are ladling pools of prepared batter from a big bowl. The batter sizzles and bubbles as it hits the hotplate. Less than a minute later, it seems, the demonstrators are flipping the pancakes over with a long-handled slice. While the next batch is being cooked, one or two of the pancakes are cut into small pieces and handed round among the spectators. We take our pieces of pancake and Thelma insists that we stay for a second demonstration.

At most of the counters in Coopers various foods are on display, but at one or two it is possible to buy paper doyleys, serviettes and even kitchen utensils and gadgets. Occasionally there is a demonstration to illustrate the properties of the latest whisk. We help to swell the group who are watching and listening to the fast talk that accompanies the procedure.

When we get back home, Thelma and I play at being demonstrators until we are called to set the table for the next meal.

Going to town and back necessitates our travelling on the number three tram car. There is a certain ritual to us catching the tram which stops at the junction of Foley Street and Smith Street just beyond Granddad's shop. In our best clothes, because we are going to town, Thelma and I are allowed to play in front of the shop and watch for the tram coming up the road. While we wait, we play at Statues or Catch the Dead Man or, if in a quarrelsome mood, at trying to tread on one another's patent leather shoes.

In Catch the Dead Man we take it in turns to be the catcher. The Dead Man has, on a given signal, to fall backwards on his heels, trusting in the catcher to prevent him falling to the ground. Statues is not much fun with only two people but I like to be swung round and, when released, to hold the pose while my partner tries her best to make me blink or smile or fidget.

As the tram appears in the distance, we race to shout through the shop doorway from which my mother emerges in her cloche hat and her neck fur with a fox's head at one end.

The passengers sit facing one another on two wooden benches the length of the tram. I am always fascinated by the "shawl women" who may board from time to time. Some of these women have baskets on their heads and I have heard them at the tram stop with their "Fresh Lemons, ten a penny." When my mother wants to explain that some event is very ordinary or some object is hardly worth having she refers to such items as "ten a penny."

My thoughts are interrupted by my mother, "How many times must I tell you, it's very rude to stare?"

"I wasn't staring, only looking."

"Then look out of the window."

I do as she says and keep a watchful eye out for my favourite posters: "Ah, Bisto!," with the dishevelled Bisto Kids, and "Guinness is good for you." My grandfather has a nightly bottle of Bass at home. It is a lovely golden colour with a head of white froth which clings to his moustache. It doesn't taste nearly as nice as it looks. If Daddy is at home, he and Granddad sometimes go out to the pub together. They come home with a bottle of stout for Mother to have as she finishes the ironing. Ironing is thirsty work according to my mother.

"Guinness is good for you." I quote and this makes her laugh.

The tram gets crowded and my mother takes me on her knee. I cannot see out of the window any more because people are standing in the aisle between the benches, hanging on to straps, fixed to the ceiling of the tram. I make the best of it by attempting to read the literature that adorns the walls: No Spitting. Fine £5; Timetable.

"Fares, please," says the conductor as he moves along. He wears a dark uniform with brass buttons and a flat, peaked cap. He carries a leather satchel slung across his shoulder into which he puts the money he collects in fares and from which he counts out the change. Hanging on a strap round his neck is his ticket punch. He inserts the ticket in a space, presses a lever and the ticket comes out with a hole punched in it at the correct fare stage. I am going to ask Father Christmas to bring me a conductor set for next Christmas. Meanwhile, I am saving the tickets so that I can play "conductors" at home. Some passengers drop their tickets on the floor of the tram and I stoop to retrieve them, for which I get, "Don't ever let me see you picking up anything from the floor anywhere. You don't know what people have walked in."

I'm a bit puzzled, "But you let me pick up a sweet that has dropped off the counter in Woolworths."

"Well, a wrapped sweet is different. But you must never take a sweet off the counter. That would be stealing."

What my mother does not know is that Thelma urges me to brush against Woolworth's sweet counter and "accidentally" knock some of the sweets on to the floor.

The tram takes us to Church Street in the centre of the town. Today we are buying new shoes. In the shoe shop we ask for Kiltie's patent leather. Granddad insists we buy good shoes. The assistant uses a buttonhook to fasten them and then we stand looking through an opening in a box which shows our feet inside our shoes and we can decide whether they are roomy enough to "grow into them". These will be my Sunday shoes until they are creased and scuffed and then I will wear them for school.

Another day we may come to buy wellingtons for walking to school on rainy days, or dancing pumps with a cluster of tiny beads on the toes. Such an array of footwear sets us above the hoi polloi who, in summer, stand barefoot at the corner of Smith Street, their feet blackened by the dirt of the pavements.

Today is special because we are going to have toasted buns in Frances's cafe in Clayton Square, to be served by our favourite waitress, Minnie Brimlow, whom my mother has known since they were girls growing up together in Edgehill. Minnie has dark hair that is beginning to grey, laughing brown eyes and large, prominent teeth. She wears the dark dress and white cap and apron that make up the uniform of all the waitresses.

"Well, I never!" says Minnie, as she guides us to one of her tables, "You get bigger every time I see you." With this, she pinches our cheeks and laughs. Everything Minnie says is exaggerated by facial grimaces. She and my mother have much to say to one another. She asks about Gerald and Mother asks about Walter. I do not pay attention to all they say because I am busy eating my toasted bun and watching all the other customers. From time to time, Minnie leaves us to attend to one of her business gentlemen regulars.

There is much laughing and joking as Minnie licks the point of her pencil before making out their checks.

We are never laden going home from town because most of our shopping is done locally; vests, liberty bodices, knickers and combinations from the Scotch Wool Shop in Walton Road, socks and gloves from Mrs Hunt who has a draper's shop in Westminster Road, thus leaving only hats and shoes and raincoats to buy in town. Cousin Nan makes our coats and dresses and school blouses, the latter made from the lengths of tussore that Daddy brings home from China. At Christmas I may be given a new, pleated skirt on a bodice and a new jersey to wear with it on Sundays. It is just as likely that I get the skirt that Thelma has grown out of.

Arriving home, we open up the lovely white shoe boxes to exhibit the new shoes to Granddad for his approval.

"Has it left you a bit short, Nan? I could let you have a couple of pounds to tide you over."

"That's good of you, Dad. I'll see you get it back when Gerald gets home."

August 1929

Daddy's ship is not coming into Liverpool. Instead, he has to "work by the ship" in Glasgow. We are on the train going up to have a week's holiday with him. Thelma and I are dressed in our gingham dresses with the fashionable waists of 1929, our school blazers and our berets. We have egg sandwiches and biscuits for the train and, to help pass the six hours, we play Happy Families. This is a card game which we often play.

"May I have Master Bun, the baker's son?"

"I'm sorry, Master Bun is not at home, but may I have Mrs. Bun? Thank you, and do you have Mr. Bun?"

I am not allowed to ask for a card unless I already have a member of that family in my hand so, depending on the answers, the player who has Master Bun can discover who is holding other members of that family, and then collect a whole family. The game can be won by the player who has the most families. Sometimes, we play on to collect whole families and it can be very difficult trying to remember who holds each family.

When we are led along to the dining car for afternoon tea the tables are set with white cloths and a tea service with the LMS insignia. In the centre of each table is what I see as a silver, two-tiered cake stand, with a bottom layer of fruit loaf and a top layer of small, fancy cakes. The waiter arrives with a tray on which are the teapot, hot water jug, milk and lump-sugar and a lidded silver dish of hot, toasted buns. It is all a great treat and, when we finally leave the train at Glasgow Central Station, I can't wait to tell Daddy all about our tea.

There are lots of hugs and kisses when he meets us at the station and, with the luggage, we take a taxi to Ibrox. We are taken to a tall sandstone tenement building, fronted by a flight of steps and are met by Mrs. Milne who has the flat where we are going to stay for a week. She makes a great fuss of us.

Each day, while Daddy goes to work, Mother takes us into the town shops. We travel into the city centre by the Glasgow underground which has a distinct musty smell, so different from the tram car. We ride with the lights on because, until we come to a station, we are looking out on black, stone walls. The driver calls out the name of each station as we draw in to the platform and, soon, Thelma and I can recite the names of these stations in order from memory. The doors slide back and then close again and we do not alight until we reach St. Enoch's.

We buy the food for our meal which Mrs Milne will cook for us and we go round the shops. To my amazement, there is even a Coopers in Glasgow. On the biscuit counter there are miniature replicas of the biscuit tins in which the loose biscuits are delivered to the shops. We buy a tiny Crawfords tin for Thelma and a Jacobs one for me. Inside each there are half a dozen tiny iced biscuits which we save to play shops with.

My favourite shops are in the Argyle Arcade. Among the many jewellers there is a shop which sells all kinds of Scottish memorabilia. There, Mother buys us each a soft roll-up pencil case in silk tartan. Thelma chooses the Royal Stewart because her favourite colour is green. I decide on the Mackintosh because it has a red background and because Mr Mackintosh also makes my favourite caramels. Further along we gaze into the window of a shop full of dolls and items for a dolls' house. A dolls' house occupies most of the window, furnished with things which are separately for sale inside. I choose the little white enamel fireplace with red foil in the grate and Thelma picks a cake stand, holding tiny cakes, just like the one on the train.

We have a doll's house at home. Uncle Sid made it. That is the Uncle Sid who married Cousin Nan, who has a sewing machine and makes our clothes. He is unemployed. Thelma and I call him Uncle Sid but when my mother talks about him she calls him Sidney Hughes. She thinks he is very ill-mannered and a shoddy workman, "always spoiling the ship for a ha'porth of tar." When Nan and Sid visit us my mother always asks, "How's Aunt Polly?"

"Moaning as usual," Sid answers while Nan blushes and smiles apologetically and again, later on when he calls Auntie Polly, "the old woman," my mother winces and gives him one of her looks. I think it's because he says "woman" instead of "lady" and he uses the word "bum" to mean "bottom," along with many other Liverpool expressions which, my mother says, indicate he is rather common, if not uncouth. I do not like his rough voice but I dislike him most when he thinks it amusing to take his hot spoon from his cup of tea and put it on the back of my hand when I'm not looking.

Sometimes, when we are tired of walking round shops or it is raining, we go into the cinema to see comedy films of The Cohens and Kellys. We see Laurel and Hardy in "Bonnie Scotland".

When Daddy is not working by the ship, we go further afield on buses or trains to Balloch or the pebbly beach at Luss on Loch Lomond, or we sail from Gouroch to Dunoon. As part of these days out we may go to a cafe where Thelma and I eat ice-cream from little silver dishes.

"I've got a strawberry in my ice-cream," I say, holding out my spoon.

"That's not a strawberry. That's a wasp."

I have my fifth birthday in Glasgow and beside my egg-cup on my birthday morning Mrs. Milne has laid a silver sixpence.

It is Saturday night. We have had our tea. The table has been cleared and the dishes washed. In the kitchen are some newly-baked fruit tarts and a meat pie. These are to be for supper because, every Saturday night, Uncle Joe, who is Granddad's brother and his wife, Aunt Polly come to spend the evening at our house. Thelma and I are allowed to stay up to see them arrive.

We have had our baths in the zinc bath , in front of the kitchen fire. We sit in our nighties, dressing gowns and slippers all ready for bed. Granddad was working late in the shop. I was standing in the bath when he came through to get his wash at the back-kitchen sink. As he came across the room, my mother turned me round to face her. This meant that Granddad saw my bottom. She always does this and I wonder why because she has said again and again how it is very rude to show your bottom and that's why you have to wear knickers.

When the visitors arrive we kiss them. Uncle Joe has a moustache, like Granddad's and I'm used to that but Auntie Polly has a whiskery chin and I would rather not have to kiss her. Uncle Joe slips a penny to each of us, "For your money box," he says.

"Now, Joe, I've told you before, you spoil them. All well at Argos Road?"

"As well as can be expected," Uncle Joe answers, "It's not the best of times for any of us."

"Only a few weeks now until Nan and Sid's wedding. Has he managed to get a job?"

"No," answers Auntie Polly, "It looks as if they'll just be moving in with us."

"Well, you can do with your Nan's help in the house," Granddad says, "We're none of us getting any younger. Seems no time at all since it was your Alf and Georgina who were living with you."

"Young Alfie was three when they got the chance of the house next door and he's the same age as your Joan, you know. He and Denny's youngest Joyce were born the same year."

"Denny and Tommy both alright?" Granddad asks about Aunt Polly's two sons before she was widowed and then married Uncle Joe.

"More than all right. They've had jobs on the railway ever since they left school. Joe saw to that."

"Well, we've got time for a game of dominoes before supper," Granddad says as, by common consent, he and Uncle Joe flip open the watches, which attached by gold chains rest in their waistcoat pockets, and check the time by the kitchen clock.

"A bottle of Bass for you, Joe, and a glass of stout for Polly. I'll pour you a Guinness, Nan, while you're upstairs, putting the girls to bed."

Mother carries the candlestick holding the candle as she sees us upstairs and tucks us into bed.

"Goodnight," she says, "say your prayers and settle down to sleep."

We wait until she is out on the landing. The adults, downstairs, can be heard laughing and talking. In unison we shout, "Goodnight, Mummy. Goodnight, Granddad. Goodnight, Auntie Polly and Uncle Joe. Hope you have a good night's sleep when you DO come to bed."

It is Sunday and, after breakfast, Thelma and I set out with Granddad for our regular jaunt to the Pier Head. We are dressed in our best, Sunday clothes. Granddad wears his bowler and carries his stick. We take the number three tramcar to its terminus. Thelma and I race down the covered walkways that slope down to the landing stage. This morning they are very steep and we have to be careful not to fall over in our best coats. Granddad catches us up and points out the funnels that distinguish one shipping line from another.

"There's the boat for Ireland (green funnels), and there's the Llandudno steamer (yellow and black). That's the Isle of Man boat just leaving, beside that dredger."

I wave to the people on board and they wave back. "Can you see a blue-funnel boat?"

"I can but I can't see its name. Yes, I can! It's the *Aeneas*. Daddy sent Thelma from the *Aeneas*. Mummy said so. I was sent from the *Antena*."

"Your Daddy usually managed to get home and see you soon after you were born."

"Why do you suppose he went to all the trouble to send us when he could have just brought us with his bags?"

I don't hear Granddad's answer because the Woodside boat has just arrived and passengers are teeming ashore as others wait to board. We know it is not "our" boat. It only goes to Birkenhead and back and runs every ten minutes.

While we wait, Granddad lets us each put a penny in the chocolate machine. Out come the slim bars of Nestle's milk chocolate in their shiny red wrappers. The boat arrives that will take us to Seacombe. Today, we are just going for the sail. If there is time we might get off the boat and walk a little way on the Wallasey side of the Mersey, but we have to be home in time for Sunday dinner.

Boarding the tram for the return journey, we can usually manage to persuade Granddad to sit on the unroofed seats at either end of the upper deck. From the seat above the driver we can race the tram in front. On tramlines we can never hope to pass it but, in our game, it counts as a victory if we reach the tram stop before the bell clangs for its departure. From the seat at the rear end of the tram when the tram behind is racing to catch us, it is our bell that has to signal us leaving the stop before the tram pursuing us draws to a halt.

From either of these seats we have a good view of operations when the electric cable has to be restored to its position on the circuit and little sparks fly in all directions. The drivers are often engaged in this activity and at these and other times they are exchanging banter as the trams separate at points or pass in opposite directions.

Sunday dinner is always special. We alternate between roast lamb with mint sauce and roast beef with Yorkshire pudding. We have roast potatoes, mashed carrot and turnip or sprouts in winter, home-shelled peas or cauliflower in summer.

"I don't want any sprouts," I say.

"I don't wish for any sprouts, thank you," is my mother's corrective reply.

"I don't wish for any sprouts, thank you."

"You'll just have one or two. That way you will grow to like them."

I know she is wrong. I never will like vegetables. I like potatoes and peas and I just have to suffer the rest.

Thelma and I hazard guesses as to what the pudding will be. To make good use of the oven, on a Sunday, my mother almost always makes fruit tarts: apple, rhubarb, cherry-plum, blackcurrant, raspberry and redcurrant. These are served with pouring custard, always Bird's. Cherry-plum or damson are my favourites because once the tiny stones are on the edge of the plate we always say the rhymes which determine whom and when we will marry. "Tinker, tailor, soldier, sailor, rich man, poor man, beggarman, thief," followed by "This year, next year, sometime, never."

Sunday dinner over, we get ready for Sunday school with our one-penny collection and our little blue books in which the attendance stamp is stuck. At the end of the year the stamps are totted up and we receive Sunday-school book prizes, adorned on the fly leaf by an illuminated sticker which says, "To Joan Lowe for very good attendance and good conduct." and this is dated and signed by the Sunday school superintendent.

The prizes vary between the unreadable *Saints and Martyrs* to *Timothy's Prayer*, to which I have been quite addicted for a considerable time. In the story, Timothy finds himself in many difficult situations. To help escape from each extremity, he says a prayer and then opens his Bible at random, whereupon the appropriate text pops up off the page for his guidance or consolation. I have tried this several times, particularly when I have broken some trinket or, rummaging in my mother's dressing table, have, unfortunately, upset her Houbigant perfume. The magic never works for me.

"Please, God," I pray, "Don't let Mummy find out it's me."

When I open the Bible I'll maybe come across a whole page of "And Abraham begot Isaac, who begot Jacob, who begot . . ." and I receive neither guidance nor consolation and have to rely on my own ingenuity to work out how to successfully lie myself out of the dilemma.

At Sunday school we sing, "Jesus bids us shine with a clear pure light, like a little candle burning in the night" and, in classes, the Misses Weeks hear us say the Bible verse which we were set to learn at home. Next we are told the story of baby Moses or Jesus, "suffering the little children to come unto him."

I don't think they tell the stories nearly so well as my mother. On winter nights she sits with us in front of the fire and tells a great story all about bad King Pharaoh in Egypt and how he was punished by the plagues. Similarly, our Sunday school prizes are less exciting than Granddad's Sunday school prizes, which Mummy reads to us from time to time. In the black and white pictures in the books the children look very ugly, but the stories about them are compelling. Despite off-putting titles like *Agatha's Trust* and *Her Benny*, they are chiefly concerned with children who lived on the streets in Victorian times, selling newspapers or matches or firewood to earn a penny to buy a hot potato to keep them from starving. Most of them got ill and died but not before they had been "saved," so they were sure to go to heaven.

We ask for *Her Benny* again and again, especially the part where the little boy is in hospital and a benevolent visitor asks, "Have you found Jesus?" and Benny's reply is, "Blimey! Is that little fellah lost again?," and we all laugh.

I know all about being saved because, not so long ago, Captain Usher came with his team to our church to carry out a week of home mission. He and his helpers all wore uniforms, a bit like the Salvation Army, only instead of navy blue and red, their uniforms were grey. Travelling with his caravan, Captain Usher toured several churches in our district and together with a Mrs. Brown and her teenage daughter, Nellie, we followed him from venue to venue.

Services were often conducted in the open air where we stood singing "There shall be showers of blessings" and "What a friend we have in Jesus" and "Blessed assurance, Jesus is mine". One evening Captain Usher kissed me. I felt very pleased at being singled out for this favour because I liked his smiling, shiny face but my mother made it fairly clear that she thought Thelma would have appreciated the kiss more than I did and I wondered why.

Chiefly, I think, as the result of Captain Usher's persuasive campaign, we all went to St. Athanasius's church to see my mother kneeling in the pew beside Mrs Brown, wearing a white headdress a bit like a nun's and getting confirmed into the Church of England, of which my father and aunts were already members.

Racing home from Sunday school in winter, we find that the fire has been lit in the upstairs sitting room. Granddad and Mother sit on either side of the fire with the Sunday papers. We are allowed to read until tea-time but only books like Sunday school prizes. *Bobby Bear*, *Tiger Tim* and *Pip, Squeak and Wilfred* annuals are forbidden on Sundays, as are also getting on with my knitting or my Knitting Nancy, both of which I am trying hard to master.

As teatime approaches, Mother goes downstairs to prepare a plate of bread and butter and thus begins the ritual of Sunday tea. We put the cloth on the large mahogany table in the sitting room with its sunshine frieze between the wall paper and the ceiling, painted by Uncle Billy, who is not a real uncle, just the husband of my mother's friend, Elsie, who died some years ago. Now he is married to Gertie McFarlane (to distinguish her from my real Auntie Gertie who is Daddy's eldest sister). As well as "little Billy," who was Elsie's son, there are George and Winnie who are the children of this second marriage and, as Mummy puts it, "thoroughly spoiled" while "Little Billy is not appreciated."

We use the best china from the sitting room sideboard cupboard to put out the plates, cups and saucers. From downstairs we carry up the cutlery, milk, sugar and the large, homemade cake, which may be rice or coconut or fruit. Thelma and I make extra trips to collect the bread and butter, the scones, the bowl of tinned fruit and either a jug of evaporated milk or Fussel's tinned cream, having taken it in turn to choose the fruit from tinned pears, peaches, pineapple or plums and, very occasionally, fruit salad. Sunday tea is quite a feast despite the fact that we have eaten the biggest mid-day dinner of the week.

After the dishes have been cleared and washed downstairs and everything put away, we settle down for the evening at the big table to do a jigsaw. Mother and Granddad often help us to do the jigsaw after, with the help of a huge dictionary, they have together filled in several copies of the crosswords in the Sunday papers and put them in envelopes ready for posting. Mother also does the Fashion Competition in the *News of the World* and Granddad fills in "Spot the Ball". Despite these regular efforts I don't think they have ever won a newspaper prize.

They do seem to have more luck with the horses, especially when the Grand National is run at Aintree in Liverpool. They talk about the horses for days beforehand while the names of the trainers and jockeys become household words. On the morning of the Grand National, Mother sits with the newspaper open at the list of runners and with closed eyes makes several stabs with a pin in order to decide which of the horses to put her sixpences on. Throughout the day this is referred to as being "on" Bonny Bright Eyes or Brown Jack or Sergeant Murphy.

Last year's Grand National was special for two reasons. Granddad had won a ticket in the Irish Sweepstake and Mother, with some friends, was actually going to Aintree to see the race. I got a bit carried away with all the excitement, so when Granddad looked at the kitchen clock and said, "Almost three o'clock, the runners will all be lining up at the tape ready for the off," I jumped up and down and begged, "Will Mummy be on the horse, now?" and wondered why my grandfather took out his big white handkerchief to wipe the tears of laughter from his eyes, before he was forced to explain that being "on" the horse did not mean she was riding it.

Mother is having a night out. She has gone to the theatre. Granddad is looking after us. We have regular pastimes when Granddad is spending time with us. One of these is Clock Patience.

Granddad deals out the cards in the twelve positions of the hours, with four cards at each. The final four cards are put in the centre of the "clock". The last card is turned up and placed in the appropriate pile. The next card is extracted from the bottom of that pile. If a king is exposed it is put on the top of the centre pile. The aim of the game is to reveal four cards at each hour before the fourth king appears. I hold my breath when three kings are displayed and each ensuing card brings a sigh of relief.

This is only one of the several kinds of Patience Granddad has taught us to play. The game ended, we climb up on Granddad's knee and we ask, "Can we dress you up like a May Horse?" We brush and comb his ginger hair and tie bows of ribbon on the strands of hair that are long enough to hold them.

"When will we see the May Procession?"

"Next week," Granddad says, "They'll be getting the horses ready this week, painting and polishing the carts and floats. Come Saturday the horses will be decorated with their streamers and garlands of paper flowers."

"Will Uncle Jack put his horse in the parade?"

"I expect so. He'll be smartening up his milk float."

"Mummy doesn't like Uncle Jack."

"Tut, tut, what makes you think that?"

"She always calls him Jack Hewitt. She says he has no manners."

"Oh, I daresay you've picked her up wrong."

We know better than to continue. Granddad never utters a bad word of anyone. We also know, from things we have heard Mother say that we haven't got it wrong. Jack Hewitt is ignorant and ill-bred, spends most of his time in the stable with the horse, and it is only thanks to Aunty Gertie, my father's eldest sister, and her business skills that the dairy in Myrtle Street didn't go bust long ago.

On wet, Wednesday afternoons, in school holidays, Granddad takes us to visit the natural history museum. The stuffed birds look very life-like, especially the eagle who has a rabbit in its claws. We stop to look at a glass case, containing a huge, ostrich egg set beside a tiny, blackbird egg. The contrast makes us laugh out loud. A door opens and a uniformed attendant appears. He recognises Granddad as a frequent visitor, raises his uniform cap and retires behind the closed door.

On summer afternoons Granddad takes us walking through Woolton woods, collecting acorns and beech nuts and pine cones. We come home with bunches of bluebells.

On bank holidays he takes Thelma and me to the pictures. Granddad likes the films that have a lot of singing and dancing. They are often called *The Gold Diggers of Broadway*. We walk up to Everton Valley and along Walton Road to the Astoria, which is a very grand cinema. Thelma and I are dressed in our best clothes and I carry my new, red handbag that I got last Christmas, and I wear my new fur gloves. Inside my handbag there is a tiny purse, an empty perfume bottle and a miniature notebook with a hinged lid of red enamel and a slot to hold a little pencil. Mummy has a notebook which I really envy. Its outside cover is coral suede. One day I find it and hide it behind one of the cushions on the couch, hoping Mother will forget about it and, as the days go by, I think of it as mine. All too soon comes the day when she says, "Guess what I found behind the cushion today. It is the little notebook I keep in my handbag, and I thought it was lost."

Mother is walking part of the way to school with us, today. She has to call in at Hunts to buy our socks. She and Mrs. Hunt will talk for a long time.

Mrs. Hunt runs the drapery shop while Mr. Hunt sits in the doorway of the kitchen, up the stairs from the shop, reading the papers. He has been unemployed for many years and there are nine children. Margaret is the eldest, at fourteen, and she is about to leave school. Then, in order of age, come Hilda, John, Kathleen, Winnie, George, Joey, Phil and the baby. We have always played with the Hunt children. One of the rooms in their house is more or less empty, except for a huge rocking horse which stands in the middle of the floor. This is where we play.

They come to our Hallowe'en parties when we "duck" for apples that are floating in a zinc bath on the floor. I hold a fork between my teeth and make stabs at the apples. Another lot of apples are strung across the room and, blindfolded, I have to try to grab one in my teeth and take a bite out of it. The prize for success in each of these games is a home-made, sticky toffee apple. We break walnuts, hazel nuts and Brazil nuts with a nutcracker and we take it in turn to throw little lumps of lead into the hot grate, coaxing them out with a poker to see if they have formed portentous shapes such as a cradle or a coffin. As a follow up to this,

Mother turns down the gas and we sit in the firelight while she reads the teacups, saying magic words as she interprets the tea-leaves to predict what the future has in store for us.

For part of the evening we play Forfeits. Each person has to put some item in the basket: a brooch, a bracelet, a ring or a hairslide. One person is chosen to kneel down with her face buried in a cushion. A second person holds the basket and, as she extracts each trinket from it, she chants, "Who does this fine thing belong to?" The child who owns the object raises a hand while the one kneeling says, "In order to retrieve this possession the owner must . . ." and this is followed by a penalty such as saying a nursery rhyme backwards, running round the room three times or singing "God Save the King".

With the Hunts we often go to play in one of the neighbouring parks. The nearest park is the Old Man's Park where there is a bowling green surrounded by benches and not much else. Stanley Park is a fair walk away, beyond Spellow Lane where we go to school. There's an aviary there with a parrot that says "Hello, Polly" and there's an ice-cream kiosk. The best park is on Stanley Road. It is called King Edward Gardens, but the gardens must have disappeared a while ago for now it is just hard-baked earth except for a few balding patches of grass. Many paths end in flights of steps to various levels so it is a good place for Hide-and-Seek or for our version of it, which we call Slaves. The slaves hide but, while the master is out hunting a slave to bring back to his den, a brave free man will risk coming out of hiding and making a rush to reach the den in the master's absence. This act of heroism automatically releases the slave who is being held captive for, unless he is rescued, he is forbidden to escape on his own.

Sometimes, in school holidays, we are even allowed to go all the way to New Brighton so long as Margaret or Hilda is in charge. We were once caught in the quicksands at Egremont, but we never told about this adventure lest the mothers imposed some restrictions on further outings.

All the Hunt family go to the Catholic church. They talk about Father Joseph, their local priest, and when he tells them to give up sweets or sugar for Lent Thelma and I do likewise. They also call their Daddy "Father" which seems odd to me because, in our house, it is always Daddy or Gerald. Even Mrs. Hunt refers to her husband as "Father".

Father Hunt sends the boys out to collect wooden, delivery boxes from the neighbouring tradesmen. He chops the wood up and puts it into bundles for the boys to sell as firewood. He also mends the shoes of all the family, so from us he buys "stick on" soles and heels.

Margaret and Hilda sometimes come to our house on their own on Friday nights when Nan and Sid visit us. We all play the games which my mother has made for us. She goes to one of the stationers in town and spends some time studying and copying the ideas. She then comes home and recreates the game in her very good copybook writing on separate pieces of card. Two such games are The Flower's Wedding and The Bird's Wedding in which the answers to all the questions have to be the names of flowers or birds. Occasionally she has to buy one of the games to justify the time she spends in the shop so we have a game called "Impertinent Questions" and another very noisy game, which we love, called "Pit". In the first of these games you are dealt a card on which there is a question. This can be something like "Are your teeth your own?" which, when your turn comes round you can ask of anyone else in the game. When you are the one to answer a question you must read out the answer on the back of your card.

"Pit" is much wilder. Each player is dealt ten cards. These can be wheat, barley, rye or oats. You have to decide which you are trying to collect so you can win by cornering the market through getting all ten of that kind of corn before anyone else can get theirs. You choose from your hand the cards that you want to be rid of and holding them face downwards you call "Two, two, two" or "Three, three, three" until someone else makes a swop with you. The cards must be of the same kind of corn. There are two wild cards, the Bull and the Bear, which you can match with any of the others, except nobody wants to part with the Bull which can add twenty to your final score and everybody wants rid of the Bear which lowers your final score.

When we are all hoarse from playing "Pit" or when the Tishy the cat is racing out of the door with her ears pinned back, we settle for a quiet pencil and paper game like Consequences or Advertisements. If we are in the sitting room we can play a great game called Escalado. We need the big table to stretch out the green

50

glazed linen track on which the painted lead horses run. We give names to the horses. Mother is the bookie and takes the bets, and she sits at one end of the table turning the handle which makes the track vibrate, and we shout out the names of the horses we want to reach the finishing line first.

The Hunt girls are well-informed about the price of margarine and tomatoes and all their shopping is done at the Co-op in order to qualify for the "divi" which, I think, is a penny for every pound spent. Mrs. Hunt does not cash her "divi" until Christmas when, each year, one child is selected for a whole new rig-out. In between they wear hand-me-downs from the older members of the family. Mrs. Hunt does all the mending and, because she has a sewing machine, she can make a little extra money taking in other people's sewing.

I wear Thelma's hand-me-downs. I get her blazers and gymslips and blouses that she has grown out of. Granddad will not allow hand-me-down footwear so I always get new shoes or wellingtons or slippers.

I have been taken to the cinema since before I could read and, then, all the films were silent.

"Why is it always raining?" I ask, looking at the image on the screen broken up by electrical disturbance. "What's she saying?" as the face of the star, in close up, fills the whole screen and words appear below her image.

Mummy's answer is usually, "Have a sweet. Suck it and see how long you can make it last."

Today is very special because we are watching a "Talkie". In it the little boy is given an umbrella for his birthday and he is very disappointed, just as I would be if that were my birthday present. Later, his father sings, "Climb upon my knee, Sonny Boy." On the screen it is still raining.

On wet Saturday afternoons we often go to a town cinema. Lime Street has the Scala and the Futurist next door to one another, and several more cinemas on the opposite side of the street. We choose the one with the shortest queue. One or other of these cinemas has a regular black and white Tom Walls comedy with Ralph Lynn and Robertson Hare. As it is a continuous performance, it does not matter if we go in when the film is halfway through. We just sit on through the entire programme of Pathe News, Cartoon and B feature until we reach the part of the story where we came in. I like to go to the Trocadero because, at one side a little apart from the main body of the stalls, there are people sitting with afternoon tea and cakes and I'm always hoping that, one day, Mummy will surprise us with one of her treats.

It is a Sunday and Mummy met us out of Sunday school because today we are going to the cemetery to visit Uncle Joe's grave. A while ago Uncle Joe was killed while working at his job on the railway. Aunt Polly will be there along with Nan and Sid, Alf and Georgina, Denny and Tommy and their wives. All the grown-ups are wearing the black clothes which they bought for the funeral. Afterwards we go back to Auntie Polly's house in Argos Road. The single front door step leads into the terraced house from the street outside. The room that we go into is small and dark. On the dresser there is a glass dome that encloses an arrangement of flowers. I don't think it is a wreath, and I don't think it is Cousin Nan's wedding bouquet for it has always been there.

Aunt Polly's house has its usual sickly smell. When I mention this to my mother, she says, "It's the bugs, they're even in the walls behind the wallpaper. These were among the first houses to be built in Liverpool. They're as old as the railway itself."

Auntie Georgina and Uncle Alf live next door to Aunt Polly so I am sent in to play with their son, Alfie, and our mutual cousin, Joyce. I never know what to say to them. They don't produce any toys to play with and they don't know how to play any games.

Joyce says, "I can count up to twenty."

I say "I can count up to one hundred."

Alfie says, "We are going on a day trip to Blackpool to see the lights."

I say, "I went on a train to Glasgow."

He says, "Where's Glasgow?"

"It's in Scotland."

"Oh, I've been there." says Alfie.

I know he hasn't but I can't think of a reply.

When Alfie came to our house my mother shared out a small bunch of grapes and we each got our share in a saucer. Alfie didn't even know what the saucer was for and spat the pips round the room. When my mother thinks I have offended by my lack of good manners, she just needs to say, "Have a grape, Alfie." and I realise I have forgotten the Please or the Thank you which have to accompany everything.

None too soon we leave for home, walking up Argos Road to Stanley Road and along Stanley Road until we reach Lambeth Road which leads down to Smith Street.

"Are they my real cousins?," I ask.

"Well, no. I suppose they are second cousins."

"What's a second cousin?"

"Your granddad and Uncle Joe were brothers. Uncle Joe's children like Alf and Nan are my cousins. Their children like young Alfie and Joyce are second cousins to my children, that's you and Thelma."

"Have we any real cousins?"

"Well, none on your Daddy's side, because his brother, Claud was killed in the war, the day before the Armistice, and his sisters have no children. Willie, my brother died at sea but his children are your cousins."

"You mean George and Dorothy? But they're grown up."

"They were born before I was married."

"George sometimes comes to see Granddad, doesn't he?"

"Well, your Granddad is his Granddad. George only comes when he's looking for a hand-out. A hard day's work would kill him."

"Is he out of work like Uncle Sid?"

"He's out of work all right but through his own fault. He had a good office job and helped himself to the till once too often. He ended up in prison."

"Did he live on dry bread and water?"

"I wouldn't know about that. From what I can gather he had a soft time of it, sitting around all day reading library books."

I think about this for the rest of the walk home. Perhaps prison isn't so bad after all. When I'm settling down to read my book, Mummy always calls me to do something like folding the handkerchiefs or setting the table or running to the top of the house to get something. On the other hand I wouldn't like to live on bread and water.

1931

"Tell us about when you were a little girl," we plead.

"For goodness sake! You've heard the same stories again and again."

"Tell about Willie and Jack."

"Of course Willie and Jack were several years older than me and they resented looking after me when they wanted to play together or go out with their friends."

"Tell about the sky-hooks."

"They were always playing tricks on me and, one day, just to get rid of me, I suspect, they said I must go to the corner shop, kept by a really grumpy old man. They said I had to ask for a penn'orth of sky-hooks."

"What happened when you got to the shop?"

"Well, he was opening drawers and climbing up a stepladder to look on shelves and getting more and more cross."

"Then what?"

"He said, 'These sky-hooks, what are they wanted for?' and I said 'I don't know what they're wanted for. My brothers said I was just to ask for them.' Then he gave me a funny look and he said, 'You're George Payne's little un, aren't you? So it's that Willie and Jack wot sent you. Well, tell them from me that next time I see them I'll have their hide. I'll give them sky-hooks.'"

"Now tell about being the horse."

"That's not a real story. It was just that the boys always wanted to play Cowboys and Indians and I got in the way. When they did agree to let me join in, it was always only on condition that I was the horse. A funnier story than that was the day Willie was going out with his friends and my mother said he had to take me with him. 'Does she have to wear that?,' he asked as my mother pulled a white woollen hat on to my head. 'It looks as if it's shrunk in the wash.' 'Shrunk or not, she's to wear it. It's a cold wind out and we don't want her awake all night with earache.'

"So, off we went and Willie met his friends. They eyed me up and down a few times and then one of them innocently asked, 'so, 'ow long 'as yer sister been out of the 'orspital, then? Ought she to be out with a bandage on 'er 'ead?'"

"What did Willie say?"

"He didn't say anything. He just let fly with his fists and said if I dared open my mouth at home to tell he'd been in a fight, he'd string me up and have my guts for garters."

"Did you tell your mother?"

"Good heavens, no! There was no point in that. She always took the boys' side. Wouldn't have believed that either of them ever did anything wrong."

"But you were Granddad's favourite."

"Oh, yes. Anything I needed it was always my Dad I asked, or Miss Viner who was my school teacher."

"Tell about school."

"It was a good school and the teachers did a lot for us for there were many families worse off than ours. I remember taking part in the school preparations for Queen Victoria's jubilee. The teachers made all the costumes and I was dressed as Britannia. Each year the school awarded a medal to the pupil with the highest record of achievement and, in my last year, I won that gold medal. That made my Dad very proud."

"Did that mean you were good at everything?"

"Heavens above, no! Needlework lessons in those days consisted of learning to patch sheets and darn socks and I was hopeless at both. Miss Viner used to bring in her best underwear and she taught the senior girls how to embroider the garments. She even brought in some of the clothes she had once worn to give to some of the poorest girls who had so little.

"My worst nightmare was knitting on four needles. I never did get the hang of it. Each pupil had to contribute twopence a week to school and sometimes I got an extra halfpenny to spend. I used to buy what we called 'stickjaw toffee' on my way to school. I was enjoying the last of it during one knitting lesson so the knitting got a bit sticky. I was in real trouble when the teacher lifted it to inspect it."

"How old were you when you left school?"

"I can't really remember. I suppose I left in the May that I had my fourteenth birthday. Had I stayed on I might have gone in for teaching or nursing, but only wealthy families could do without the wages that their children could earn. I went to work in Burman's office. They were tailors and I learned how to keep the books. I worked there until I was married. That wasn't my first job. Before I left school I helped at Watson's dairy. That was when we lived in Edgehill and the dairy was opposite Granddad's shop. I went out with the delivery man who drove the milk float, carrying the big metal milk churns. It was my job to knock on the doors and collect the jugs that people brought to the door. We used a pint measuring can on a long handle to reach down into the churn and fill up the jugs. For helping every morning before school I got sixpence a week.

"I used to get invited to spend regular evenings at the Watsons' house. Mrs. Watson was widowed and her unmarried sister lived with her. They used to bring out a planchette — that's a board with letters round it. We three sat round it and they would ask questions. There was a pointer that moved to the various letters which supplied the answers to their questions. When my parents found out what was going on I had to make excuses to refuse further invitations from the Watsons. That wasn't too difficult because often I had to deliver boots that my Dad had repaired for a customer. Also I had started going to a class where we trained to give displays with Indian Clubs."

"And sometimes you went out with Minnie."

"One time I remember. My brother, Jack, was working as a projectionist at a local cinema. He gave us two free tickets. There was always an interval while the reel was rewound and the next one set up. Minnie said she was hungry so we left the cinema to buy chips at the nearby shop. Holding our chips in their newspaper wrappers we then attempted to re-enter the cinema only to be stopped by the doorman. 'And where do you think you're going?' Our explanation was not to his liking so I said, 'Get Jack Payne here. He knows we're not telling lies.' Presently Jack appeared. He was very embarrassed by the whole affair and never again did he give us free tickets."

"Yes, but you still went out with Minnie."

"Once two chaps took us to the theatre. We sat in the box seats that overlooked the stage. I felt very grand especially when an attendant appeared in the interval asking if we wished to order coffee. I had never tasted coffee before but I was quite prepared to act as if I drank it every day, except that Minnie let me down by saying, "Coffee! 'aven't you got any lemonade?" That wasn't the worst moment of the outing. That was yet to come in the water scene, a great speciality in those times. Everybody was tense in his seat as the heroine struggled in the water. Minnie was carried away by it all. From our box she stood up and yelled for all to hear, 'Look out! she's drowning'. I was so ashamed of this exhibition. I don't think our escorts were too happy about it either. They didn't ask us out a second time."

We never tire of the tales Mother tells. They are better than anything we read in books.

Granddad never talks about his childhood but Mother says that there were five boys and one girl and they had a cruel stepmother. She regularly found reasons for the boys to get beatings and Granddad, who was the eldest, took the worst of them. My mother blames the beatings for the infection that set up in Granddad's leg so that he now has to walk with a stick.

When Granddad was twelve he ran away from home. He walked the several miles out of Liverpool to St Helens, which in those days was farming land. There, a man took pity on him, gave him board and lodging and taught him his own craft of shoe-making. Mother says proudly, "He's not a cobbler. He's a real shoe-maker. When I was young he owned five shops. Now, there's only Smith Street left and we moved here after my mother walked out on us. I think she went back to her own family home. I don't know and I don't care."

Thelma and I have walked up to the recreation ground at the top of Lambeth Road. We call it "the swings" but there is also a tall slide, several see-saws, a shaddle and a roundabout. The row of swings consists of two kinds; the baby swings which have slots to ensure the young child cannot fall out and the big swings for which there is always a queue.

We wait our turn but we have never learned how to jerk our arms and legs to get started so, each time the swing comes to a stop, we are dependent on one another or someone else to give us a push. Other children swing, two to a swing, spitting out pomegranate seeds at the same time. One sits in the swing and the other stands astride her, working the swing up to, what seems to me, a great height. I'm envious and wish I, too, could go as high. I did, once, allow a big girl to stand astride me on the swing but, enveloped by her skirts, I could only see her knickers so I couldn't experience the flying sensation and the whole thing was so claustrophobic that I felt sick and never took up such an offer again.

I want to go on the slide but when I climb up to reach the top, I cannot find the courage to release hold of the rail and slide down, and it isn't easy descending the steps with children on every step refusing to move out of the way.

On the see-saw, Thelma is heavier than me and we cannot get it off the ground. I stand watching the roundabout for a long time. It is a circular board, with rails at intervals and this revolves round a central, iron stem. The idea is to grab one of the rails, push it hard to start the action and race along beside it until you can jump aboard. I tried this once and skinned my knees on the gravel. When Mother found out how I had fallen, the roundabout, like standing on the swings, became forbidden.

When we leave the swings we go into the library. You have to be aged seven to join so I have just joined. None of the books have pictures and the librarian restricts me to the young readers' section so I choose titles like *Mr. Bunny's Surprise*, *Sandyman's Tales* or *Animal Stories*. By accident I come across a jewel like *Beyond the Blue Mountains*, but nobody has told me to look at the name of the author to repeat such a prize so

I only look at titles. Recently I read *The Scamp Family*, so I can follow this up with *The Scamp Family on Holiday* and *The Scamp Family Grows Up*.

At home I can now read books that Thelma has been given for birthdays or because she was ill at the time. Thelma had her tonsils taken out when she was seven. She was not allowed to be put to sleep under an anaesthetic and she said she saw all that went on. She has had rheumatic fever and she has a weak heart. When we caught measles and chicken-pox she was more ill than I was. The only thing I enjoyed having all to myself was whooping cough. Mother said it would probably do me the world of good to breathe a bit of sea-air, but nobody could be spared to take me further than the street corner where the road was being repaired and I was told to breathe deeply to inhale the fumes from the molten tar.

Thelma's books are *What Katy Did*, *What Katy Did Next*, *What Katy did at School*, all the Dimsie books, stories of the Chalet School and *Little Women*.

When I get home, I will read my book or play with my collections of scraps and cigarette cards. There is a friend of the family called Bob Brightman who sometimes drops in. He works for a tobacco firm so he brings us lots of cigarette cards. We collect footballers, all in their different coloured shirts, but we know nothing about football.

Everyone got very excited round here when Everton won the cup. We sang songs about Dixie Dean and he got carried through the streets of Liverpool. I only know about this because we were taking Auntie Lucy and her friend, Mary Bentley to the station to make their return journey home after a brief day visit. We could hardly get to the station for the crowds.

Mary Bentley, who has a strong Derbyshire accent and has rarely been outside her home village of Old Glossop, looked wide-eyed at the crowds, "Ee!" she said, "Where will we all get on Resurrection Day?"

As well as footballers we collect pictures of film stars and I am gleaning much information from my latest card collection of fresh-water fish. With this collection there is even a book in which to stick them but, as Mother pointed out, how could we read what it said on the back of the card if we stuck it in a book. She took the book and cut out all the oblong insets and made price tickets for when we play "shop".

If Mother gives me a penny or two to spend when we are in Woolworths, I buy a packet of scraps to add to my collection. I don't stick these scraps in my scrap book. I like to spread them out on the table, deciding which are my favourites.

Most days, Thelma and I walk to school unaccompanied. It takes us about half an hour as we usually dawdle, looking in shop windows and playing games.

We cross Foley Street which divides Smith Street from Westminster Road. We pass the police station, which we call the Bridewell, and Mrs. Hunt's the drapers. There's a hairdresser's where Mother sometimes goes for a cut or a wave. Most of the time she wears her long chestnut hair in a low bun on the back of her neck or, occasionally, in earphones. In the hairdresser's window is a golden figure seated cross-legged in Buddha fashion. Spikes protrude from its head in all directions. "Have beautiful hair with a Eugene permanent wave", it says on a placard above it. I think the statue is quite ugly and I can't believe anyone would want to look like that.

There's Bowler's the greengrocer and Harriman's the butcher. Nobody I know has a telephone although I have a toy one, so each day Mr. Harriman sends his messenger boy, in his long, blue-striped apron, to our shop where he delivers the meat that Mother ordered on the previous day. He collects the order for the following day. We request such things as "a pound of chuck steak, minced and two lamb kidneys" or "a sixpenny rabbit and half a pound of best stewing steak" or "three lean, double loin chops".

Between the shops there are a few houses whose front door steps lead right on to the street. Mrs. Scully is frequently outside, monkey-stoning her front step. She scolds us for playing in the puddles.

"Making more washing for you poor mam," she says. "White socks, indeed! They won't stay white for long."

Half way along Westminster Road we pass the public baths. The baths are a kind of landmark on our route to school.

"The rain didn't come on till we reached the baths," we say.

"My apple lasted all the way to the baths."

"We won't eat the next sweet until we get to the baths."

There's a toy shop which, for most of the year, displays a poster which reads "Save in our Christmas Club". In the window are dolls' houses, prams and cradles, a rocking horse, teddy bears, dolls, Hornby train sets and bridges and towers constructed with meccano kits. I've never owned a doll's pram such as those in the window. They look just like real baby prams. Mine is a very small one, made of tin and painted blue. I am not allowed to wheel it round the block. In the shop doorway or just in front of it we sometimes play with a hoop, ball or top and whip, according to the season. I have a skipping rope but I have never mastered skipping nor bowling a hoop nor getting a top to spin.

We spend our Saturday pennies on the way to school. We usually make our purchases from the Barlow Lane sweet shop, where all the sweets are displayed in the window. I choose toasted coconut caramels. I get five for a penny. Thelma buys scented cachous, very small sweets which make your breath smell nice. When I give her one of my sweets, she gives me one of hers, which doesn't seem very fair.

Towards the top of Barlow Lane the shops peter out and we have to find other diversions. We take it in turn to walk on walls. They are only two or three bricks high but I often fall off and I have permanently scraped knees. We play at making long strides from one pavement stone to the next playing "Tread on a black line and you'll marry a nigger." I have never seen a black person, but I do know about them because Mother has read us parts of *Uncle Tom's Cabin*. There's some half-caste children that we sometimes see on the opposite side of the road. They have big brown eyes and dark, curly hair which I envy.

A man shuffles along the pavement who Thelma says has sleeping sickness. I ask her what that is and she says, "Use your brains, what do you think it is?" We pass a polio victim in a wheel chair but I remember that one mustn't stare and look away. There's a boy who walks very slowly with his legs in irons and he has to throw each leg forward in turn so that, at each throw, I think he is going to overbalance. Another man always shouts to us. Thelma says we are not to answer because he is soft in the head which is the same as being not all there and we hurry past.

At last we reach the busy Walton Road that crosses the top of Barlow Lane. We stand on the pavement and watch the policeman, on point duty, directing the traffic. Presently he comes across, collects us and sees us across to Spellow Lane. Spellow Lane has big houses behind high hedges or walls so there's little to look at before we reach school.

Outside school in gold letters there's a plaque that reads "Westminster High School". Nobody ever calls it anything but Spellow Lane school or "The Daft School", the latter, I think, because we have our share of pupils who might not fit into the larger classes of other schools in the district.

We wear school uniform — navy and gold, velour hats, reefer coats, gymslips and blouses in winter and panamas and blazers with gingham dresses in summer.

In winter, there is a coal fire in each classroom, for the school is a large, converted house consisting of four classrooms. Miss Grasby takes the intake of youngest children. As soon as I could read and write I moved into Miss Blair's class.

Miss Blair is an old lady with grey hair who looks after an invalid sister at home. When we went on a visit the sister was sitting up in bed and every so often she reached for a cup at the bedside and spat phlegm into it. Mother says this is because she has bronchitis but she'll probably outlive her sister, who not only cooks and carries up all her meals but teaches as well. I knew Miss Blair before I went to school because when Thelma was seven we bought a piano and Miss Blair comes to the house, once a week, to give her lessons.

It is a beautiful piano, made of dark rosewood and Mother is "paying it up". Granddad is not in favour of the "never, never", but he does enjoy Saturday nights when Auntie Muriel plays the piano and other aunts and uncles stand round, singing "After the Ball is Over" or

Daisy, Daisy, give me your answer, do.
I'm half-crazy, all for the love of you.
It won't be a stylish marriage,
We can't afford a carriage,
But you'll look sweet upon the seat
Of a bicycle made for two.

If Daddy is home, he and Mummy sing together, "If you were the only girl in the world and I was the only boy". Granddad treated Auntie Muriel to some sheet music copies of the modern songs; "Red Sails in the Sunset", "Dinner for one, please, James", and "When I grow too old to dream", although he himself prefers the songs sung by Richard Tolber and Gracie Fields because "They can sing". He has one or two of their records which he plays on a wooden cased gramophone with a turntable. It is wound up by a side handle and you have to keep renewing the needle. The records are easily scratched but still recognisable among those we have are, "In a Persian Market" and "Rosemarie, I love you". I have a special party piece which I am allowed to perform at these evening parties before I go to bed. Granddad taught me the song and I dress up in pyjamas and with the help of Granddad's bowler hat and cane I parade up and down the sitting room singing

As I walk along the Boys Belong with an independent air,
I can hear the girls declare, "He must be a millionaire".

At school I no longer use a slate. Miss Blair lets us write in exercise books which we buy from the school shop. We also have to provide our own pens, pencils, rulers and blotting paper. If you do good work, Miss Blair sticks a red paper star on the page. Ten red stars gain a silver star and this gets stuck at the back of the jotter. Ten silver stars gain a gold star and I already have three of these stuck in my sum book.

We have special books which we take home for practising our handwriting. On the top of each page is a line of printed copybook writing, followed by a page of ruled spaces in which we try to reproduce the same strokes. My mother, who has won prizes for her handwriting, cannot understand why Thelma and I write so badly. "They don't seem to teach you how to hold a pen properly," she says. When she feels the need to go up to school to complain about the number of articles which Thelma has lost in successive weeks, she decides to mention that she cannot even read Thelma's attempt at writing.

"My dear Mrs. Lowe," says Mrs. Sharp, the headmistress, "When could you ever read a doctor's prescription? We are here to foster intelligence and self-reliance in our pupils, not to waste our time on trivia. Good handwriting is not in itself a sign of intelligence. As for your other complaint, Thelma must learn to take responsibility for her own property."

My mother repeats this for the benefit of anyone willing to listen over the next few weeks. She sniffs to show her disapproval.

Later on I will be in Miss Stewart's class. She is young and wears her golden hair in earphones. Miss Ethel Sharp, one of the headmistress's daughters, teaches the top class. Sometimes we sit at the desks in Miss Sharp's classroom while, accompanied by her sister, Edith, at the piano; Ethel conducts our singing in rehearsal for the Wallasey Eisteddfod. We sing "Up the airy mountain, down the rushy glen, we daren't go a hunting for fear of little men", "A froggy would a wooing go" and many more songs. I cannot sing but we will all be part of the choir that enters for the festival. This happens every year. We attend in freshly laundered blouses and pressed gymslips, our hair having been washed the night before. We sit in our appointed places until it is our turn to line up on the platform. There are some adult choirs and solo performers and so we sit for a long time. I'm not very interested in the songs that are sung but the mannerisms and the facial expressions of the performers keep me amused. In the intervals between items I enjoy mimicking the gestures and thus engaging the interest of those who sit beside me. I do not listen to the remarks of the judges and we never win, but we do get a special mention as the youngest choir and I enjoy the applause.

When we sit in Miss Sharp's classroom, I watch John Phillips who is the tallest boy in the school and wears long grey flannel trousers. He never looks in my direction because his eyes are fixed on Dodo Smith who is very pretty and almost grown up. All the other boys are in short trousers with matching jackets; Tommy and Harold Wilson who both have blonde, curly hair; Harry Harris who wears horn-rimmed glasses and always has his hand up to ask silly questions of the teacher; Andrew Tucker who sits by himself because nobody would choose to sit next to him. He has runny ears and they smell. There is a girl called Dorothy with a very bad scar on her neck where she had a thyroid operation.

Two girls have recently enrolled in the school whom Thelma and I join every day on our journeys to and from school. Their names are Muriel and Doris and they are the same ages as us. Thelma and Muriel are both very bossy. They make Doris and me walk in front of them so they can whisper and giggle and tell secrets. Sometimes they deliberately tread on our heels. Mr. D'Arcy, their father owns the swimming baths at Linacre Lane — well, I think he's the manager which is the same as the owner, and the family live on the premises.

Muriel and Doris invited us to visit their home one day after school. We had our tea with them and, after tea, when the baths were closed to the public, we played at racing round the empty baths, shrieking our heads off and hearing our shrieks bounce back at us from the walls. It was exhilarating. There was no one telling us to be quiet or to behave like little ladies and I was aware of a sense of freedom, never before experienced in the close confines of home. I wish we could live at the swimming baths.

There is no playground at our school. When we have a morning break we all line up in the school kitchen to be served with a small beaker of milk and two biscuits for which we pay either a penny or a halfpenny, depending on the size of the beaker. The small beaker is a little bigger than an egg-cup and the larger beaker is a little less than twice that size. The milk is warmed in the winter and the biscuits are always either Marie or Arrowroot. Both kinds have ornamental edges so it is part of the ritual to nibble round the rim first before taking larger bites out of the remaining circle.

We never have any form of physical activity except for a couple of months of the summer term when we trail down to the Westminster baths for a swimming lesson. I share a cubicle with another girl, and the two of us have to find room on the two pegs and single bench to put all our clothes and towels. The panama hats and blazers fill the hooks so our other clothes are piled in a heap on the on the bench and usually end up on the stone floor, which is already wet from the former occupants.

Lining up on the edge of the pool is followed by gingerly lowering oneself down the steps at the shallow end and clinging on to the bar along the width of the bath. As each person comes down the steps one has to inch along the bar to make room for her. By this time we are all shivering because the pool is not heated so we are urged to jump up and down to get our shoulders wet. This, we are told, will stop us shivering. It doesn't.

The lesson consists of hanging on to the bar and trying to lift one's legs off the bottom, which exercise is succeeded by standing in the water and imitating the teacher's breast stroke movements which she demonstrates fully dressed, from the safety of her position overlooking us. Some pupils are fortunate enough to catch the looped end of a rope which, from the side, the teacher throws into the water. They experience the feeling of swimming as they are dragged through the water towards her. I look forward to enjoying this some day but there is only time for two or three children to get their turn at this. Next, the teacher organises a race where, in the water we walk the width of the bath. In conclusion we enjoy a few minutes free activity before the whistle sounds and we all climb out, dripping.

My teeth are still chattering when, back in the cubicle, I find the biscuits that Mother put in my blazer pocket. It takes me a long time to try to dry myself with a towel which has been lying on the wet floor, and even longer trying to get wet socks on to wet feet. Eventually, I emerge to wring out my swimming costume, hand knitted by my mother. I do this too close to my feet so by now my shoes and socks are soaked.

By the time the next swimming session comes round, I have a bad cold and am only allowed to stand at the side and watch. This is so frustrating. I know that if I were only in the water I would find that, this week, I could swim.

In the winter school exercise takes the form of instruction in ballroom dancing. The school hires Swainson's ballroom for the last hour of Friday afternoons. For this I wear the beaded dancing slippers that Mother bought for me in town. One Miss Sharp plays the piano while the other Miss Sharp chants the rhythm of the waltz, the vleta or the military two-step that we are learning at the time.

From our dancing lesson, Thelma and I walk home along Walton Road. We pass Haddons, the fishmongers, where we had to call this morning on our way home from school at dinner time. Then we had to collect the fish for our Friday dinner. We bought three-quarters of a pound of skate which mother poached to accompany the mashed potatoes. We also bought salt fish which Mother and Granddad will eat for breakfast. This morning we cut down Fountains Road to the bakers where, because we hate fish, we are allowed on Fridays to buy a special treat. This is their speciality of small sponge cakes, iced and sprinkled with coconut with half a cherry decorating the top of each. They are seven for sixpence but we always buy four for threepence ha'penny. We carry them home in a white cardboard cake box. Mother usually keeps the box for a week just in case it comes in handy for something. I think that, like me, she thinks it is a bit too good to throw out with the rubbish.

This afternoon, just for a change, we stay on Walton Road all the way to Everton Valley. This entails passing Meeson's sweet shop. The window is full of chocolates. Thelma draws my attention to the notice in the window which says "Chocolates 4d a quarter and a quarter free". Thelma says the sweets we buy are two ounces for a penny. She says when you buy a quarter you get twice as many. She works out that if we save our Saturday pennies for two weeks, not next Friday but the next after that, we can have enough money for each to have a quarter of chocolates. I'm a bit worried in case the chocolates turn out to have cream instead of caramel filling for then they wouldn't last for long. On the other hand, when we buy sweets we have to pass them round at home. You get five caramels for a penny so you are left with only two for yourself. If we just have to pass the chocolates round once when we take them home, we would have more for ourselves, even if they are creams, so I agree.

A little while ago Mrs. Jones, who has the chandler's shop just across from the lamp that stands beside the public lavatory on an island at the corner of Smith Street, asked Mother if Thelma and I would let her daughter, Lillian, walk to school with us. Thelma doesn't want to do this because she says Lillian is an only child and that's why she is a spoiled brat. Lillian is a little younger than me. She has big brown eyes and ringlets so you would expect her to look pretty but she doesn't because she always has her mouth open. I'm not sure whether she has perpetual catarrh or whether she suffers from adenoids but her nose is always red and I feel a bit sorry for her. She spends most of her time crying so her nose gets even redder and Thelma says nasty things to her which make her cry more.

Thelma says we don't have to feel sorry for her because her parents must be very rich, because she has a yoyo that cost half a crown. Thelma and I have tin yoyos that cost twopence each which is probably why the string is always breaking, and it's hard to keep them going. Mrs. Jones often slips us a penny but Mother says she is a neighbour so we have to refuse the penny. Sometimes Mrs. Jones gives us an ice-cream cornet which we don't have to refuse and once she gave us each a new sixpenny yoyo. They are made of wood and have cord instead of string. We play with them on the way to school, counting how many times we can make them go up and down and doing tricks like throwing them over our hands or, best of all, "taking the doggy for a walk", when you have to let the yoyo run along the ground and then continue going up and down.

My mother never lacks the zeal and ingenuity to invest certain days of the year with a kind of magic so we anticipate them for weeks in advance, knowing always what form the rituals will take.

With Christmas and Boxing Day over we look forward to the New Year, and long before we are allowed to stay up to "See the New Year in" we are encouraged to make New Year resolutions. These, over the years, range from promising not to complain when its bedtime to resolving not to comb our hair in the kitchen and to dust our own bedroom. Roast pork with sage and onion stuffing and apple sauce is always served on a New Year's Day and, in the afternoon, Granddad takes us to see "The Vagabond King" at the Astoria.

On February the fourteenth — St Valentine's Day — we do not associate the day with sweethearts and cards but with presents. After tea, we stand at the sitting room fireplace, shouting up the chimney "Look out! Look out! for Mr. Valentine". There's a rap on the sitting room door and we dash to open it. There is no-one there but a parcel is lying on the landing. We tear off the brown paper wrapper to reveal the present. It has a certain familiarity about it but we are too caught up in the excitement of the moment to give this much thought. Back again to the fireplace, a repeat of the chant and the knock and another parcel arrives by magic. Many years will elapse before we are let into the secret which is simply that my mother, thinking there are far too many presents for us to appreciate fully at Christmas, whips one or two away to a safe hiding place from which they emerge to brighten up mid-February.

It is Pancake Tuesday. Thelma and I dash home from school at mid-day. We use a pestle and mortar to grind the granulated sugar into the fineness of caster sugar while Mother stands, frying pan in hand, making each pancake as we are ready to eat it. It gets tossed and flopped on to the plate, sprinkled with lemon juice and sugar and rolled up ready to be dipped into the mound of sugar at the side of the plate. Each pancake is the size of a dessert plate and we eat six or seven each until we can eat no more. The last drop of batter is used to coat slices of apple so we end the meal with apple fritters.

When Easter arrives, all the aunts and uncles give us chocolate Easter eggs. The egg from Auntie Polly is my favourite. The silver-foiled egg has a strip of cardboard in front of it in the shape of a church door and standing in the doorway are two miniature celluloid figures. The groom has his morning suit and top hat painted on but the bride wears a dress and veil of real net and I keep her among my treasures.

On Easter Day, Mother either dyes or paints faces on the breakfast boiled eggs. At Easter one must wear something new, even if it is only a pair of socks lest, according to local lore, the birds will seek you out as the target for their droppings. Thelma and I usually acquire new Sunday hats for Easter. They are bucket-shaped, straw hats, decorated with satin ribbons and rosebuds.

We must wait a little longer for the official arrival of summer. Ascension Day declares this so, even if it is pouring we go to school in our summer dresses, short white socks, blazers and panamas. It is a day we celebrate with a half-holiday.

May Day brings the horse parade to Liverpool and, throughout the month, children organise their own Saturday processions through their local streets. Each procession has its Queen of the May, even though her train may be only a remnant of old lace curtain. Passers by give the children coppers and the rag-and-bone man finds this an opportune time to make his appearance, giving pennies or a balloon in return for a jamjar or a bundle of old clothes. The day is brightened further by a tune from the organ-grinder, his monkey receiving most of the attention and causing people to throw pennies out of their open windows before he moves on to the next street. On such occasions I wish we were allowed to play outside with the street children. As it is Thelma and I have to content ourselves by watching all the goings-on from the sitting room windows.

We are allowed to go up to Everton Valley and stand with the pavement crowd to watch the Orange Procession at Whitsuntide. Heading the parade is the uniformed figure of the man swinging the mace. He is followed by the drums, cymbals and brass bands and the children in their white outfits with orange sashes. Woe betide anyone who attempts to cross the street while the parade is in progress although my father, brought up in Norwich and ignorant of these sectarian rituals, once attempted to do just that. As he describes it, he thought the man with the mace was about to strike him down.

Empire Day arrives bringing another half-holiday from school. In morning school we sing "God Save The King" and "Land of Hope and Glory" and race home at lunchtime, waving our rag rectangles of Union Jacks.

Mother has gone for her annual day sail to Llandudno. She sits in a deck-chair and reads a book for the whole day. She looks forward to getting away from Smith Street for a day. Because it is Sunday, Granddad is free for the day to look after us.

After the mid-day meal, Thelma and I go up to the bedroom to get ready for Sunday school. I cannot reach my straw hat on the top shelf so I stand inside the heavy oak wardrobe, raised about a foot from the ground by a drawer in its base. Unaccustomed to such abuse the wardrobe lurches forward, the door closing on me trapped inside in darkness. Just as its momentum is about to send it crashing to the floor, it is caught by the side of the bed in its path. I hear Thelma scream and Granddad rushing up the double flight of stairs as fast as his gammy leg will allow. From my prison I hear the exaggerated "dot and carry one" of his tread and this, together with the suffocating smell of camphor, serves to dramatise the situation. He and Thelma push the wardrobe upright and I emerge, unharmed. Wiping the sweat from his brow and with no intended blasphemy he exclaims, "My God, child, I reckon your guardian angel was with you today." In my usual fashion, I take his words literally and from that day on, through most of my childhood and beyond, I am certain that a miracle has saved me from death. In Sunday school I sing with gusto, from this personal experience, "We are on the Lord's side. Saviour, we are thine".

But not that afternoon. Granddad says, "That's enough excitement for one day. You've had a nasty shock. You can forget about Sunday school. Just have a quiet lie down with a book." There is no chastisement just this unexpected treat. I feel very important and not in the least shocked so I thoroughly enjoy the rest of the day, unblighted by Sunday school attendance.

I am eight years old when the next miracle occurs. As a special treat, Mummy and Daddy have taken Thelma to London for the weekend. I am not considered old enough to accompany them so I stay at home with Granddad. Friday night, along with Wednesday night and sometimes Monday night, is Granddad's night for going to the pictures, the programmes changing twice a week and there being two cinemas, both just across the road. It is Friday night and, with him, I go to the Garrick, on the corner where Lambeth Road and Westminster Road meet. There is a double bill. The first film is Peter Lorre in *The Hand*, a frightening film in which his hand, acting independently of his own wishes, leads him to commit many crimes. The second film is about a fortune teller who predicts how each character will meet his death. About half-way through the film, I am watching this man standing on the edge of the platform as the train steams through the station. I know he is going to fall in front of it on the track and I shut my eyes tightly. The next moment Granddad is holding my hand and, unbelievably in the middle of the film, we are leaving the cinema. I don't know whether somebody pushed the man under the train or whether he jumped there himself and I don't suppose I will ever know.

In bed, by myself, without the usual company of Thelma, I have a nightmare re-living the events of the two films. I wake up in the darkness too frightened to go to sleep again yet afraid to lie awake in the darkness. I think, "If only there was a candle or a nightlight on the bedside table." More from faint hope than from faith in an Almighty, I sit up in bed and feel around on the table.

When I find the nightlight in its saucer of water and the matches beside it, I light it and, eventually, fears eased, I fall asleep. Of course I know it's a miracle but I don't tell anyone about it for fear lest "my miracle" is reduced to an everyday occurrence.

The family return from London and I hear about the Tower of London, the crown jewels and the Beefeaters. Thelma tells me later how very tiring it was walking round and the bit she most enjoyed was sitting in the cinema watching *Calvalcade*.

1932

In the school summer holidays we are frequently taken out for the day, wearing our school blazers, short, white socks, sandals and berets instead of panamas, the one concession to casual wear.

Going to New Brighton is my favourite but sometimes we take the tram car to parks such as Sefton Park, Bowring Park, Calderstones and Woolton Woods. We take a ball so that we can play on the grass, and we collect bunches of wild flowers to take home and keep in a jamjar. I can recognise pink and white clover, yellow buttercups, daisies, bluebells and scarlet pimpernel. We don't care for dandelions. We make daisy chains and we hold a buttercup below the chin to see whether its reflection will declare that we like butter. I am always looking for a four-leafed clover or a shamrock to bring me luck.

I'm a great believer in luck, both good and bad. I know it's bad luck to put shoes on a table or open an umbrella in the house. It is bad luck to walk under a ladder and I dread breaking a mirror because that would bring seven year's bad luck.

My mother, unaware that by so doing she blights my life, continually quotes all the superstitions that her own mother heeded.

"You've bumped your elbow? Bump the other one quickly or you'll have bad luck."

My elbows are permanently disfigured.

"A pimple on your tongue? You must have told a lie."

I wonder which of my lies has earned the pimple.

I keep hoping that we revisit the park which, under a glass dome of a roof, had a combined sweet shop and cafe. One day, in a thunderstorm, we sheltered there. Mother bought some sugared almonds but I was disappointed that we didn't sit down at a table to be served with ice-cream in a silver dish on a stand. I think it was the same park that has the cuckoo clock. The "clock" is made of growing plants and you hear the cuckoo at each hour. Thelma says it isn't a real cuckoo but I know it is.

We have been to the sands at West Kirby and Hoylake. The sands there are beautiful but it takes a long time to get there and sitting on a tram car can make me feel sick. Mother suggests that I take a library book to read. I'm into fairy stories now so I choose books like *Irish Fairy Tales* or *Tales of the Norsemen*. With my head bent over a book I feel sick more often. We sometimes have to get off in the middle of the journey to breathe a bit of fresh air. We wait a few minutes for the next tram along the route and we don't have to pay a second time for Thelma and I each have a child's summer penny transfer ticket on which you can have four rides.

Mother keeps the tickets when we go out with her, but if we do the same trips with the Hunts each has to look after his own ticket. If you lose your ticket, you have to keep back a second penny to get back home, so you can't buy sweets or lemonade. When this happens we stand around at the tram stop or rifle through the litter bin hoping that someone has discarded a ticket that has not been punched four times. Mother has said that if ever you lose your tram fare home, just give the conductor your name and address so I say "Let's buy the sweets and then, when we don't have any money left we can do as Mother says".

"Don't be silly, " Thelma says, "Mother didn't mean you can do that."

"It's like telling a lie," says one of the Hunt girls, "You'd have to tell Father Joseph in confession."

"You don't have to tell him."

"If you don't when you die you'd burn in hell fire. Besides, it might count against John. He's got to get accepted to study for becoming a priest."

I bear this in mind next time Mother is talking to Mrs. Hunt in her shop.

"John not helping you serve today?" Mother asks.

"No," says Mrs. Hunt, "John won't be helping in the shop for a while. We found out John was helping himself to the till."

My mother would have liked to be a nurse. I think she would have been a good nurse because she makes it possible for her patient to really enjoy being ill and kept in bed.

She brings in breakfast on her own special tray which is blue enamel with a cane edging. On the tray is the tiniest of teapots with milk and sugar basin to match and a rack of the same china to hold the slice of toast. It is a white china breakfast set decorated with blue flowers and Granddad helped us buy it for one of Mother's birthdays.

After breakfast she brings up the jug of hot water and I stand on wobbly legs getting washed in the toilet bowl on the washstand. While I wash, she puts clean sheets on the bed, liberally sprinkling the pillows with her Florida Water or Eau de Cologne. She splashes this on the clean handkerchief to help me breathe better through my stuffed nose. Finally she puts my favourite annual on the table and brings me a wooden tray so that I can do the latest jigsaw.

One winter, Mother, Thelma and I all had 'flu at the same time. Mother had the bed brought down to the sitting room and we lived and slept by the fire for a week. I liked sitting in bed in the firelight with Mother telling us stories. It was my idea of heaven.

Thelma has to stay in bed. She has rheumatic fever and this is the second or third time she has had it. There is a couch made up like a bed in the sitting room where she lies most days to make it easier for Mother to run up and down the one flight of stairs.

I go to school on my own and I do all the messages. Mother is always thinking up special treats for Thelma which I usually share. Today, on my way home from school, I've to go to Sayer's cake shop on Walton Road to buy two chocolate Othellos. They are choux pastry filled with whipped cream and topped with chocolate icing, a bit like chocolate eclairs except the Othellos are round. In the shop I can't remember the name of the cakes I am to buy so I point to them and say "Two chocolate Romeos, please." The shopgirls think this is a good joke.

Sometimes, after I get home from school, I cross busy Smith Street to Hannah's, the grocer's to buy one quarter of boiled ham or a packet of Velveeta cheese for Granddad's tea. We have to buy some things from Hannah's as well as Sharp's because they are both customers of Granddad.

We buy our bread from Peter's at the corner of Smith Street and Foley Street. It is really called Taylor's bakery, but we call it Peter's because Peter is the shop assistant who has served there as long as I remember. When I was very little he used to toss me in the air and catch me as I came down. One day, when he was about to throw me up as usual he said, "You stand over there by the biscuits, Thelma, and when I throw Joan, you catch her." I wouldn't have trusted Thelma to catch me. She can't even catch a ball. I wriggled free and, after that, I settled for Peter just swinging me round with my feet off the floor. Peter gives me the large, Pilot loaf that we always buy, and he also gives me one of his pink wafer creams which he knows is my favourite.

Our back yard leads out on to an alleyway that links the backs of all the shops on our side of Smith Street. We call it the entry and it is a bit smelly because it is where the bins are kept. Some children play in the entry but we don't play there as there may be rough children. I am allowed to use the entry as a short cut to Reeces, where occasionally I am sent for a baked custard or a scone for Granddad's tea if the scones my mother baked a week ago have run out.

I go home daily for my mid-day dinner. More than once, on very wet days, Dr. Foster, having called to see

Thelma, has taken me back to school in his car. It is a Baby Austin and, because he is very fat, he can only just squeeze into it. These are the only times I have been in a private car. No-one else I know owns a car but some of the girls in school boast about knowing someone who knows someone else who has a car. To keep my end up I talk about our next-door neighbour, Mrs. Lapin, who has been to America.

Very occasionally we go away for part of the school summer holiday.

One year we went to stay for a few days with Auntie Lucy in Old Glossop. Auntie Lucy is the second wife of Granddad Lowe who died before I was born. Like Auntie Polly, she has a whiskery chin. We went to the open-air market and Mother bought us sandals. We saw Auntie Lucy's friend, Mary Bentley serving at her father's pork-butcher's stall. We bought a pork pie, some brawn and some black puddings. On the Sunday we all went to church and Auntie Lucy introduced us to her friends as "Gerald's wife and daughters". We also went long walks in the area round the village.

The best holidays of all are the years we rent a bungalow in Heswall. We have rented it for a month this year because Thelma needs the fresh air. Mother packs a huge, black cabin trunk and we take card games and books for wet days. The bungalow stands at the edge of a field so we can play outside all day when it is fine. On hot days we run around in our cami-knickers and we use the huge parasols to shield us from the sun if we are sitting. They are made of a kind of oil-skin and have a sweaty smell.

Most mornings, Thelma and I do the long walk down to the village shops to collect the messages. We always linger at the sweet shop to watch the machine in the window that is winding the sugar into hanks. Its two metal arms hold the sugar as if it was knitting wool and, as they revolve, it is beaten into a smooth, cream rope of caramel. Inside the shop they sell the cream-coloured candy balls made from this caramel. They are very light in weight and they melt into the tongue. There's a toy shop, too, and this morning I am going to spend the five shillings that Granddad gave me for my birthday. I am going to buy a sand-set, a collection of shallow, tin moulds to fill with sand and turn out in various shapes of fish as illustrated on the lid of the box.

Mother is cooking a big dinner today because Auntie Muriel and Auntie Gertie are coming for the day. They wear their long-skirted dresses with fashionable drop waists and the chenille berets crocheted by Auntie Muriel. After dinner we all do the long walk to Gayton beach. It is very hot but I am cool because I just wear my knickers and my sleeveless striped grey and yellow dress. It takes a long time to walk along the footpaths and climb the stiles that lead to the beach, so there's not much time to play. The water is a long way out so we can't paddle but I can make the shapes with my sand-set. The sand is a bit sugary and they don't turn out exactly like the ones on the box. Mother shows us how to dig down to reach the clay below the sand so we end up making shapes out of the clay and, at Thelma's insistence, this becomes a baker's shop.

On fine days we gather blackberries on the common. The common is a large expanse of wild fern and brambles and it is quite hilly. Mother makes blackberry tarts with the fruit that we collect.

It is still light even after tea so Thelma and I play outside with Dorothy and Mildred, two little girls that we met the last time we stayed in Heswall. We play at "Families". Mildred and I, who are the youngest, have to be the naughty children and Dorothy and Thelma are the parents who smack us. Because we are naughty children we answer back, and when we are sent to bed, we get up and run away. It is all great fun, a bit like it was when we were playing in the empty swimming baths, discovering the tremendous sense of freedom when play is unrestricted by the presence of parents. Perhaps it is assuming the identity of someone other than myself that is satisfying and releasing and exciting all at the same time.

On Wednesday afternoons and on Sundays, Granddad spends time with us at the bungalow. He takes us walks and we collect caterpillars and put them inside matchboxes. We feed them with leaves and wait for them to turn into Red Admiral or Tortoiseshell butterflies. One night I lay awake listening to the creature beating its wings inside the matchbox. I was too frightened to let it out because the sound so resembled the hateful, big moths that beat their wings against the oil lamp which gets lit after dark. When I opened the box the next morning the butterfly was dead. I did not collect caterpillars again.

Sometimes, there are very heavy thunderstorms. The dark sky is suddenly lit up by a flash of lightning. I find it exciting. At such times, when we cannot go out, Granddad and Mother teach us to play poker. We each pay a penny for a dozen cowrie shells and with these we make bets. I learn to recognise pairs, runs, flushes, three and four of a kind and a full hand. At the end of the game we cash in our shells and this means you might end up with more than the penny you started with. Poker is much better than Snap or Patience.

1933

Thelma and I have a great game that we play called "Mannequins". The idea came to us as we sat through a mannequin parade with Mother. There are regular mannequin parades in the big stores and you don't have to pay. When we came home, we begged some old petticoats, blouses and shoes from Mother and we dressed up and walked around as the mannequins did. We played it that way for many weeks but there came a wonderful day, after which it became quite a different game.

Daddy made friends with the widowed stewardess on one of the ships. She had two teenage daughters, called Doreen and Heidi. She invited us to tea one day. After tea, we four girls went into a small room where there was a sewing machine. We sat round a table and

Doreen and Heidi introduced us to the game they played.

They had two tiny dolls, each about five inches high, with what looked like real hair. Their limbs moved so they could easily be dressed and undressed. Each doll had an extensive wardrobe of clothes in materials such as I had never seen before, all in the prettiest of colours. The dolls had party dresses and ball gowns made of silks and satins and velvet. They had little fur necklets and muffs and all manner of fancy trimmings in swansdown, net, ribbons and rosebuds.

The girls explained how their mother had taught them how to fashion these garments and accessories from the scraps of material left over from the sewing she did for passengers. Once again, I enjoyed being free to play with other children in a separate room, away from adults.

When Mother at last gave in to our pleas, Thelma and I became the proud owners of two small dolls, similar to those we had played with. We christened them Doreen and Heidi and, to have an excuse for continually disrobing them, they became our mannequins.

We don't have the exotic materials that we so envied but Cousin Nan sends us her scraps. Satin, silk and velvet are replaced by cotton sateen, rayon and velveteen. Neither Thelma nor I can sew but we drape and pin the scraps of cloth round our models and we are well satisfied with our efforts.

There will come a time, many years later, when I choose to learn to sew. It will not be school needlework lessons which foster this hobby. Rather it will be the fond memories I cherish of dressing those tiny dolls.

Our favourite game is "Shops". There is no greater treat than Mother announcing that she is going to be busy for the day making jam, bottling fruit or spring cleaning and so we can have the sitting room to ourselves for the whole day. The best part of all this is that we can set up the shops on the big, mahogany table and we don't have to "clear the table" to make space for the next meal.

We have a sweet shop which we have had as long as I can remember. It has small jars, sealed by corks, and bigger jars with glass stoppers just like those in the real sweet shops. I don't think it was new when it first became ours, because the contents of most of the jars have become solid and wont shake out, but we buy dolly mixtures and miniature liquorice allsorts. These are the sweets which we weigh out on the toy scales with tiny weights made of real brass. We have added to the sweet shop a little slot machine that dispenses chocolate neapolitans. It is a replica of the chocolate machines that stand on the sea-side piers. I think we were given this as a money box. Mother does not encourage us to set any store by money boxes. She says children shouldn't be looking for people to give them money, be they friends, relatives or neighbours. You have to insert a penny in the top of the tin before the drawer will open to deliver the chocolate, but we have discovered how to take the back off, so we can keep using the same coin. We also have a miniature cash register just like Ernie Sharp's.

The grocer's shop was new when it was given to us. Mother was able to buy it from a toy shop that had a "closing down" sale, so she got it cheap. Unlike the sweet shop, which is really a shelved, cardboard box with a flap to help it stand upright, our grocer's shop is made of wood, painted in white enamel. The back wall of the shop displays about thirty, pull-out drawers, each with a raised porcelain label attached to the front, saying RICE, SUGAR, TEA, SAGO, FLOUR, etc., and Mother has given us all the various contents. We do not weigh out the flour or the cocoa because they would make a mess but we do weigh out the rice and the cornflakes. Mother made us little bags into which our scoop will fit. When we clear up, these can be emptied back into the drawers. There is a pretend clock on the wall of the shop, above the drawers, and there is a separate counter to hold the scales. Best of all, fixed to the front of the wooden sides of the shop are two shelved, glass windows. Of course they are not real glass, Mother says it is a called Mica, more flexible than glass to make it fit round the curved shelves, exact copies of those you see in the most modern shoe shops. On the window shelves we display miniature packets of Oxo, Symington's soups and Jacob's cream crackers. We take it in turns to serve at each of the shops because, unless Mother is sitting with us, somebody has to be the customer.

Another sitting room game, which we play, is cooking on what we call real stoves. The tin stoves have holes in the top, over which we place the little aluminium pans that Mother bought in the same sale. Short pieces of candle or nightlights stand on the base of the stove under the pans. When lit, they heat the water in the pans. Mother gives us a potato and an apple and, if we chop them up very small and wait a long time, we have stewed apple and mashed potato to serve on our miscellaneous tea-set plates.

When there's not enough time to set up shops and stoves, we play imaginative games. I am Margaret Dickey-Bird and I am eleven. Thelma is Hilda Brick and she is fourteen.

We also play "Roundheads and Cavaliers". This game is a bit more boisterous and has got us into trouble more than once. We ride on the bolstered arm at the end of the couch which sits below the big sitting-room windows overlooking Smith Street. In my fervour, I knock down the big plant pot, holding the aspidistra on the window sill. It falls on my forehead and Mother is worried I will be scarred for life. I am but it doesn't show under my fringe.

When the arm of the couch has to be mended and we no longer dare risk it for rides, we find an alternative in the cupboard doors of our big, oak sideboard. The doors are strong enough to take our weight and we swing back and forth. My mother would be very angry if she ever discovered that we so misused her precious sideboard. She bought it, second-hand, when she was first married. It has a large central and two side mirrors. Below its top shelf are two small cupboards with stained glass doors, supported by carved wooden pillars.

A friend, called Bill McFarlane, who is a decorator, came one year and made our sitting room very smart. He papered it in a light, brick-coloured paper and above the paper he painted a sunshine frieze, shaded orange to peach throughout its depth.

Our sitting-room looks especially grand at Christmas. There is always a giant Christmas tree standing in a tub at the window. Each year we add just two extra ornaments which Thelma and I are allowed to choose from Woolworths. All the baubles are made of very fragile glass and, inevitably, at Christmas parties when we play "Musical Chairs" and "Blind Man's Buff", some get broken and we shed tears. Our most precious are the large balls in pastel shades of pink, blue and green on which have been painted large clusters of dark cherries. Over the years we have collected a number of smaller glass balls in various colours and some ornaments in the shape of Father Christmas and elves. The tree is hung with tinsel and little, twisted red-wax candles, which will be lit later, are clipped on to the outer branches.

Paper garlands are hung from the gas bracket in the centre of the ceiling to reach the walls. They are the concertina type and get kept from year to year. We have coloured paper bells, balls and lanterns which, when unfolded, hang, in clusters, from the corners of the room and over the fireplace. The holly and the mistletoe will be added on Christmas Eve when, as late as nine o'clock, they will be sold off cheap.

I can't wait for Christmas. It is an eternity from one Christmas to the next. The preparations start weeks beforehand when we sit round the kitchen table at night, seeding raisins, picking stalks off currants and sultanas, chopping almonds and candied peel to help Mother make the mincemeat, the puddings and the cake.

In the week before Christmas is the great day when the postman brings a dozen mince pies from Aunt Alice. Daddy lived with her after his mother died and this is her annual present to the family. The mince pies are individually wrapped in parchment paper and packed in a box so that they arrive intact all the way from East Lynn. Should one, accidentally have got broken we are each allowed to have a few of the crumbs. The pastry, unlike my mother's, is so short and rich that it crumbles in the mouth.

Ernie Sharp receives a specially big order from us, at Christmas. This order includes three tins of biscuits, one assorted creams, one chocolate biscuits and another of Crawfords' Tartan shortbread. The first of these tins will not be opened until Christmas Eve but it is splendid just to look at the stickers on the bottom of each tin, which illustrate the assortment within. We spend ages anticipating which biscuit we will select when the tin is opened. I am always torn between the pink cream wafer and the round cream biscuit with its red centre of sugar-coated jelly.

Mother comes home from town with books which she has bought for the children of her relatives. She covers the books with clean, brown paper and she either reads us the stories from them or we may, ourselves, be allowed to handle them during the run-up to Christmas, when the covers will be removed and they are given as presents.

Thelma and I sit, each evening in the gaslight, knitting iron-holders and kettle-holders which will be our presents to all the aunties who give to us. Although my mother is not a sewer, she is very adept at copying ideas for presents from the objects we bring home from school handwork.

While in the first two classes we made beads from strips of paper, torn from out-dated wallpaper pattern books, now we cover strips of stiff cardboard with the wallpaper and, having masked a matchbox with a strip of border paper, we stick it on the covered base and make what we call a matchbox holder to hang on the wall.

We have a school exhibition of work, each year, to which the parents are invited. Here they see parrots in colourful felt which form tea-pot holders, or nightdress cases made up of many paper petals in two shades of pink — two opposite corners of a crêpe-paper rectangle are wound round a knitting needle and ruched to make each petal while the uncurled side is sewn to some cheap lining material such as sateen. There are handkerchief cases where a little china bust of a lady is caught on to a base which is then covered with strips of inch-wide ribbon, placed in layers, to form a crinoline. My mother buys similar materials for us to recreate these objects at home and, only then, discovers that our handwork was accomplished as we stood at the teacher's desk, watching her hands create it.

Similarly, Westminster High School, or Spellow Lane School as we call it, boasts in its prospectus that French is being taught. We do have lessons in French when we stand up and read from a Longman's text book about Charles and Marie and their parents. Thus I discover that la plume is the pen and le crayon is the pencil. I only recognise these words from the printed form and when I read them aloud, no-one ever corrects my completely English pronunciation.

Miss Stewart, our class teacher does not work the sums on the blackboard as Miss Blair did. That is for babies. We each have an Arithmetic text book in which there are chapters entitled Long Division, Fractions and Decimals. We are all at different stages of this book so there is no class teaching. The regular procedure is that, on reaching a new chapter, you go up to the teacher's desk. Indicating the first page of examples Miss Stewart explains that this is the way to set down all the exercises that follow in the same chapter. I'm very good at setting them down in my exercise book and, always looking back at page one of the chapter, I follow the clues that result in the correct answers. By this method, I've coped with long division and fractions. I'm finding decimals more difficult, but I've realised that one can manage perfectly well to get the correct figures in the answer by completely ignoring these little dots which they call decimal points. Putting the point in the answer once the sum has been worked presents no problem as I just insert it at random, much in the way Mother picks horses for the Grand National. When the teacher marks my work she does not ask me to read my answers. If she did she might discover that I have not the slightest understanding of notation. She says, "Well done, you've got it all correct but for the decimal point." She inserts this with her red pencil and gives me a tick to show I succeeded. It is not in this school that I find out that any mathematical processes are related. In a similar fashion we also "do" Algebra.

For Geography and History lessons, we read round the class from text books and sometimes the teacher dictates whole paragraphs that we write in our notebooks. To anyone reading my notebook it would appear that I have some understanding of the effect of the Labrador Current and the Gulf Stream on the climate of Britain, when my sole achievement is an ability to read and spell the words.

We are given nightly homework and the only homework I really hate is copying maps. Having traced the map of the world with messy, blue tracing paper, the countries must be coloured, chiefly pink to indicate the extent of the British Empire. The seas also have to be painted. The colours run and there isn't time to let the paint dry in order to draw in all the rivers and names with a black-ink mapping pen, so everything runs together into a big, smudgy mass.

I am not unhappy at school. There are good reports to take home each term which indicate marks in the eighties and nineties. Because my mother is so proud of me, she and Granddad buy a new wooden jigsaw and they write on the box "To Joan, for good examination results. June 1933", in case, when we are all sharing it, I might forget that it is really mine. Occasionally it is a more personal present. I have a very fine silver chain — well, perhaps it is not real silver because it is turning black — and it is so fine that it often twists into a knot which only Granddad can unravel. Granddad stresses the qualities of patience and taking one's time. On this chain, I alternate the black and white replica of Mickey Mouse and the coloured, enamel golliwog that we received when we had collected and sent away enough labels from the jars of Golden Shred marmalade.

Of course, the best presents arrive on Christmas morning. Stories and poems tell about children hanging stockings at the foot of their beds but Thelma and I hang pillow-cases. Thinking about the pillow case at the foot of the bed makes it even more difficult than usual to go to sleep on Christmas Eve.

There are many nights when it is not at all easy to go to sleep in 86 Smith Street. Quite apart from all the laughing and talking that goes on below us on nights when visitors are entertained, there are many times when political meetings are held round the big, gas lamp that stands beside the public lavatory at the end of Smith Street, where Lambeth Road, Westminster Road and Foley Street meet. These meetings go on for a long time and they are very noisy.

Granddad says, "What can you expect? It's that good-for-nothing Mosley along with his good-for-nothing Blackshirts."

Diagonally across from Granddad's shop, in the opposite direction from the lamp, are the tram sheds.

The trams run well into the night and restart early each morning.

Once the candle has been blown out, the street lights, shining in through the window, ensure that I can still see the ceiling where the damp has penetrated the plaster and formed shapes in which I see the faces of threatening half-human monsters. Even when I fall asleep I have nightmares when they reappear.

We wake up early on Christmas morning when it is still dark. Seizing the filled pillow-cases, Thelma and I toss aside the flat, square boxes, the usual handkerchiefs from Auntie Polly and Auntie Georgina, to find jigsaw puzzles, the newest *Bobby Bear* or *Pip, Squeak and Wilfred* annuals and tiny presents of objects to add to our doll's house and shops.

I have only twice been disappointed with the main Christmas present from Mummy and Daddy. The first time was the Christmas I received a doll's cot. It wasn't that I did not want a doll's cot but months before I had found it hidden under a bed in one of the spare bedrooms. When it was given to me, it was no surprise and I resolved that, in future, I would avoid all wrapped parcels in the run-up to Christmas. The second time was when my present was *The English Book of Common Prayer*. I'm pretty sure Mother gave us each a copy the year she was confirmed. I had to struggle hard to keep back the tears of disappointment. I was six at the time.

At the bottom of the pillow case are the tangerines and rosy apples and a little, gold, net bag of foil-wrapped chocolate coins. As it gets light we sit in bed, eating the goodies and reading the new books.

When we go downstairs there are more family presents, such as the two, large bun-loaves which, each year, Auntie Polly mixes for us before taking them round to be put in the oven at the local bakery. There is a box of crackers passed in from the Lapins, next door, and a tin of caramels left for us by Mr Mann, with the curly hair, who works for Granddad. Even without Mother's constant reminders, we know that we are two of the luckiest children in the world.

We have roast chicken for Christmas dinner, served with parsley stuffing and bread sauce. Thelma and I pull the wishbone. I always wish for a toy sewing machine or typewriter. The pudding has been on the stove since breakfast. When it is carried in from the kitchen, Granddad pours some brandy over it and sets it alight, making the blue flames dance all round the plate. We have it with rum sauce which makes it harder to find the lucky charms that have been hidden in the pudding until they are in the mouth. There's a bachelor's button, an old maid's thimble, a little bell and several, lucky, threepenny bits. We finish by pulling the crackers. As well as a paper hat, and a motto or riddle there is a novelty of some kind. I would like to find a ring but I am satisfied with a red, cellophane fish which curls up in the warm hand and then bounces all over the table as if it were alive. Mother lets me collect all the scraps of crêpe paper from the crackers along with the paper-figure scraps that decorated the front of each cracker.

Once the meal is cleared away, dishes are filled with tangerines and caramels, and the boxes of stuffed dates and crystallised fruits, given to us by neighbouring shopkeepers, are opened. I beg for the box with the open front that held the tangerines and this I set up on its end on the table. I use the largest pieces of crêpe paper to make the stage curtains and parade my little paper figures to and fro as the characters I saw in last year's pantomime. This is better than any of the presents in the pillow case.

While I am playing with my toy theatre, it is the scenes from *Sleeping Beauty* which are in my head. I think about it nearly every night when I am in bed. In the final scene, before the curtain came down, all the princes are lined up on the stage, each dressed in a different colour, their tri-cornered hats matching their skirted jackets. Since then my favourite colour has been coral pink.

It has been known for our family to go in a taxi to the pantomime. Perhaps the taxi took us home, but taking taxis was a dream of mine not often gratified.

"Mummy, there's a taxi," I say, as one passes us, walking home late and tired from Auntie Polly's.

"See the red light." Mother says. "That means it is either occupied or it is already booked. We'll just keep walking but you look at each taxi that comes along and, if it has no red light, then we can ask the driver to take us home."

My mother is rarely lost for an answer and truth is no obstacle. Thelma and I dawdle on our way home from afternoon school.

"What kept you?" Mother, dressed in hat and coat, wants to know. We invent excuses.

"Very plausible, I must say," Mother comments, using one of her favourite phrases, "I remember telling you to hurry home from school today."

"We forgot."

"You'd both forget your heads if they were loose. And here I was all ready to take you to town to have tea and toasted buns in Francis's."

"You never said."

"It was meant to be a surprise."

"We can still go, can't we?"

"Now? When it's nearly five o'clock? It's out of the question. How could we get home again in time for Granddad's tea? I'll slip upstairs to take off my hat and coat. Thelma, you go across to Hannah's for a quarter of best Cheshire cheese and you, Joan, get the cloth on and start to set the table. Next time I tell you to hurry home from school you might remember."

Mother having gone upstairs, Thelma says, "When did she ever take us to town on a Monday? It wouldn't surprise me if she hasn't still got her washing apron on under her coat."

For the next week, we hurry home from school only to be met with "Good, you can fold the handkerchiefs ready for ironing" or "You're just in time to finish drying the dishes, while I pop into Nurse McKinlay's".

Thelma and I join the Band of Hope. We sit at classroom desks in a local school. We sing songs, watch lantern slides and recite the promise again and again. We return home.

Mother says, "Getting home at nine o'clock at night! I've never heard of such a thing. You won't be going there again."

It is the last Friday of the Christmas term, so our normal dancing lesson is to be a fancy dress ball. Parents are invited. Prizes are to be awarded for the prettiest, the funniest and the most original costumes. Thelma has a hired Bo-Peep dress, a big picture hat and a crook. With her ringlets hanging down below her hat, I think she will probably win the prize for the prettiest. I am a bit disappointed in my costume. Mother cut down an old pair of men's trousers but they are still too big for me. I wear an old shirt of Granddad's, a pair of braces and a bowler. Mother paints a moustache on my face with burnt cork and I carry a walking stick. She says I am to be Charlie Chaplin and I must do a funny walk in the parade. She thinks I might win the prize for the funniest costume. As it turns out, neither Thelma nor I come home with prizes.

Today we are going to Blacklers. Blacklers is a very grand shop selling among other things, towels and sheets and tablecloths so it has that fresh, clean smell that cotton has before it goes into the wash for the first time.

A central marble staircase on the ground floor leads up to a platform where it separates, left and right, into two further flights. From the upper floors you can look down through banisters into the central well. From the ceiling above hangs a huge artificial parrot on a perch. Thelma won't look down because she says it makes her dizzy. She prefers the stores that have lifts. I hate lifts. Just before it is going to stop at each floor it gives a lurch and my tummy does a somersault and I think I am going to be sick.

We will perhaps buy half a yard of ribbon to trim a hat. Our money is taken by an assistant at the wooden counter. It is put into a round, wooden box along with the bill. The lid of the box is screwed on. This is dispatched on pulley wires, criss-crossing above our heads. It is received by a cashier, sitting suspended in a kind of cage. She sends it back to the counter with the stamped receipt and our change. I never cease to be amazed by the miracle that gets each box back to the correct customer.

Once a year we go on the Sunday School Treat. All the mothers accompany us on the charabancs. We call them "sharabangs". We trail long, coloured paper streamers out of the windows and sing songs all the way to Raby Mere. We sing "One man went to mow, went to mow a meadow" and "Ten Green Bottles". Mother carries egg sandwiches and our teachers pass round big tins of sweets.

When we arrive we line up in classes to get our drinks of cold milk and our sticky buns. In between the races we dash back to Mother for an egg sandwich or a banana. There are swingboats at Raby Mere but I am too frightened of being sick to do other than enviously watch the abandon of other children.

The day ends with the Mothers' Race and we stand cheering, hoping Mother will win. There are no streamers left to wave on the trip home but we repeat all the same songs.

1934

I am reading a book called *Winning the Victory*. It may have been a Sunday school prize but not one of my prizes. It is all about idols. The idols are not graven images like the Israelites made when Moses left them at the foot of the mountain. Instead they are many different, ordinary things like favourite toys, clothes or even chocolate bars, that a family of children have grown to worship as idols because these things have become so important to them. One day the selfish children resolve to make amends. They save up pennies for a long time and just when their mother most needs it, they present her with a small fortune.

I think this is a good idea so for a while now I've been taking the odd copper that gets left on the kitchen dresser and secreting it away in the red handbag that I had when I was little. I'm considering hiding the handbag in the walk-in cupboard, in the spare room where we keep our toy shops and stoves.

Mother seldom goes into this cupboard and, from time to time, when she decides it has to be tidied, it is Thelma and I who have to do the tidying. This usually takes us a whole afternoon. One reason for this is that on the cupboard shelves there are many books which the ship's passengers have left behind and Daddy has brought home. Most of them are by Warwick Deeping and we dip into them to see if they are interesting.

One book is very exciting. It is all about a woman who is badly treated by a man in her bedroom. He does dreadful things to her like taking off her nightie. Thelma says it is better not to tell about reading the books. She said the same thing when we found something under a bed in a box labelled "Douche".

I said, "What's it for?"

She said, "It's for washing your fanny."

I said, "What's your fanny?"

She put on her big sister look and said, "If you have to ask then you are too young to be told."

I think that douches and fannies are things that Thelma and her friend, Muriel talk about on the way to school when they make Doris and me walk in front of them and deliberately tread on our heels.

The cupboard seems a good place to keep the handbag.

It is some weeks later and on our return from school Mother greets us with, "It has been my lucky day, today. Guess what I found when I was clearing out the cupboard in the spare room. I found this old handbag of mine with one and ninepence in it. I can afford to treat myself to a new hat."

I am both astounded and appalled at this announcement. I was saving the money for her to rescue her from ruin and now she has found it when it will only buy a hat.

Thelma says, "I suppose it was her money."

I say, "I don't care if it was. It certainly wasn't her handbag. She had no right to open it."

Two nuns regularly appear at the shop counter. They sail in wearing their billowing black habits and wide-winged, white head-dresses. Sometimes Mother invites them in for a cup of tea. One sits, nodding and smiling, while the other does the talking.

"Mr. Payne is a saint, so he is. There's nobody goes away hungry from his shop. It's certain the Almighty is looking down this day and saving a place for your father in heaven beside him."

In my mind I see a picture of a bearded old man in the sky, peering down between the clouds with my granddad sitting beside him, wearing a golden crown and playing a harp.

The image changes when Mr. Cotton, the new vicar at Saint Athanasius, calls. As he leaves he says, "My next stop is Great Homer Street."

My mother says, "You can catch the number three tram outside the shop door."

"It's a fine day, I think I'll walk. I can have a chat with God along the way."

Suddenly, God has become much less holy and quite approachable. The holiness aspect is renewed when Good Friday comes round. It is like having two Sundays in one week. The shop is closed as if it was a holiday but everything else is closed too and there is nowhere to go. We are not allowed to knit and we have to eat fish.

May 1934

Since I can remember, Auntie Muriel has been the skeleton in our family cupboard.

She is the younger of Daddy's two elder sisters. According to my mother, Aunt Alice, the aunt who sends us the Christmas mince pies, looked after the Lowe family following the death of their mother when they were children. Muriel was always the delicate one so, while Gertie went to business and my father went to sea, Muriel was kept at home. In one of her pitying moods, my mother will say, "Poor Muriel! She never had a chance. Just used as a drudge."

Auntie Muriel has the same slight frame, sallow complexion and almost black hair as my father, except that her hair has patches of iron-grey and is cropped into a shingle. Her close fitting, neat-collared, long-sleeved silk suits and fine woollen dresses resemble in style, if not in quality, the fashions we are later to see in newspapers and newsreels, worn by Wallis Simpson, the constant companion of the Prince of Wales. On my Auntie, they serve rather to accentuate her bony neck and wrists and protruding collar bones.

Because she is anaemic, she has to eat uncooked liver and switched raw egg, and because of this condition perhaps, she finds most household jobs too taxing. It can take her a whole morning to dust a bedroom or peel the potatoes. On such occasions, Mother, in a less than charitable frame of mind, will say, "she could do with a bomb behind her." Granddad is never impatient with Auntie. He has bought her some more sheet music to play on our new piano.

She is happiest sitting working at her very fine crochet lace. We have her handiwork displayed on our best Irish linen tablecloth in the form of a deep pointed border, and she has decorated many church altar cloths. She can sit silently for a long time at this work, absorbed in her own thoughts and, apparently, oblivious of the conversation around her so that when addressed directly she will give a little, bird-like start — this is because of her "nerves".

She can manage to cope with putting seams or hems on curtains and with turning and mending sheets and pillowcases, and for this reason we have recently invested in the latest hand-operated, Singer table sewing machine. Mother hoped to get her interested in sewing for herself, so the paper pattern and dress material were purchased from Lewis's in town. Daily, between meals, the material was laid out on the kitchen table. Pieces of pattern were pinned according to the accompanying diagram, but Muriel couldn't quite bring herself to risk the first cut with the scissors. Despite my mother's efforts to "chivvy her along", it was all too much for her and the project had to be abandoned.

Auntie Muriel is tidying her dressing table drawers. Everything litters the bed and the floor. She steps backwards on to a slim book of prayers with the face of Jesus in colour on the cover.

"Auntie," says Thelma, "You're standing on Jesus."

Auntie Muriel jumps all of a foot into the air and, later, she has to lie down to recover from the shock.

In Liverpool, for a long time, now, they have been building a tunnel under the River Mersey. It will mean that cars will be able to go via Woodside to the Wirral Peninsula or via Seacombe to the rest of Wallasey. It will be quicker than driving down to the Pier Head and travelling by ferry. King George V and Queen Mary are coming to Liverpool for the official opening but, so that people without cars get a chance to see it. Next Sunday, before it opens to traffic, members of the public are to be allowed to walk through it. Auntie Gertie and Auntie Muriel are going to join the hundreds who plan to make this excursion. Mother says, "Good luck to them. Just about anything could go wrong. Imagine the panic if the lights fail and all you have to think about is the hundreds of tons of water on top of you. Just five minutes of that would be enough to put Muriel back in Rainhill."

Mother's worst forecasts do not come true, but neither do the aunts emerge unscathed. On one of the many metal studs, in the floor of the tunnel, Auntie Muriel trips and injures her knee. As a result, she becomes a complete invalid for the rest of the month.

It is May 1934 and, because Auntie Muriel spends alternate months with Auntie Gertie and with us (that is of course when she is not away having a rest at Rainhill or Lancaster mental hospitals), this month she is staying with us.

A letter from Jack Hewitt informs us that Gertie, now approaching her fifties, is on the brink of a nervous breakdown.

"That's no surprise!" is my mother's comment, "Living with Jack Hewitt is enough to give a saint a nervous breakdown."

It is decided that, at Jack Hewitt's expense, Mother will accompany Gertie on a week's holiday to cheer her up. They travel the short train journey to a Derbyshire village called Hope.

Thelma and I, together with lists of instructions which include directions as to when we will change our underwear, are left with Granddad who is perfectly able to cope with the main tasks such as cooking. He sees to it that we set and clear away the table, wash dishes and do the shopping. Auntie Muriel somewhat vaguely and twitchingly behaves much as she normally does. This entails hours in the bathroom, changing her dress several times a day and sitting with the mending or her own crochet. Even so, each day, her behaviour becomes a little more erratic. With the shop to run, Granddad is too busy to notice these symptoms and, in my mother's absence, they are to pass unobserved by any adult until the day when everything explodes.

It is a Wednesday and the shop is closed for the afternoon. Granddad says that, as it is a lovely day, we will take the tram car from Everton Valley all the way to the terminus where we can walk the country lanes.

We always enjoy this because Granddad points out plants such as Deadly Nightshade which look lovely but cannot be touched as they are poisonous. He uses his stick to uncover a scarlet pimpernel or rats' tails or a ladybird. He lets us pick wild flowers and even stop at a cottage for a glass of milk.

Granddad is sitting in his chair. Thelma and I, dressed in our school blazers and berets are waiting, as we always are, for Auntie Muriel to come downstairs. She finally appears, all powdered it seems, except the powder is bright pink, the bright pink that Thelma and I recognise as Colgates tooth powder. If Granddad notices he says nothing except to look a bit sharply at Thelma and me, whispering and giggling together. The look indicates to us that it would not be wise at this point to share our observations and we set off.

All goes well on the outing until Granddad is reaching up with the handle of his stick to pull down the overhanging branches of hawthorn so that we can gather it. This upsets Auntie Muriel.

"Woe to him who gathers May, E're Christmas come he'll rue the day," she quotes.

She has even more to say when we take it inside the house on our return.

"Now, now, Muriel," Granddad says, "There's nothing to get upset about." With this, he tries to settle her in a chair.

Auntie Muriel pushes him away. "Don't make advances to me," she shouts, her arms striking out in all directions, "I'm a pure woman!"

"That's alright, Muriel. You'll feel better after a cup of tea."

"Bugger off. I don't want your bloody tea," and there follows a string of oaths and accusations, during which Grandad stands, confused and helpless. Only his flashing eyes and his heightening colour reveal the struggle between his normally placid nature and his urge to defend himself against this onslaught. He is quite short and ducks most of the physical blows, taking advantage of the occasional, momentary respite to utter, hoarsely, "Now, now, Muriel, calm down. Take a hold of yourself."

Thelma and I stand, fascinated. We frequently hear adults argue, but this is high drama. Granddad suddenly becomes aware of our intense attention.

"Thelma, go and tell Nurse MacKinlay that Muriel isn't well and we need her to come in."

Two minutes later, Nursie arrives, all big, bustly and strong. She takes charge. The first thing she does is to dismiss us upstairs to the sitting room, with instructions not to come down until we are told.

Dependent only on our ears to follow the course of events, we are aware of raised voices, of furniture being knocked over, of doors opened and banged shut. Footsteps indicate someone leaving the house. We dash to the sitting-room windows and see Ernie Sharp crossing the road at speed. He goes into Hannah's opposite, the only neighbours with a telephone. Then whoever had left the house to enlist his help returns and there ensues a period of quiet. This is too much for our curiosity. We tiptoe to the door and venture out on

115

to the landing. We crouch there for a while, peering through the banisters, hoping to catch some sound or glimpse of the goings-on, one floor below. We are considering inching round to the top of the stairs when everything seems to happen at once.

There is a hammering on the shop door and more than one pair of heavy footsteps pounding through the shop and up the half-dozen bare wooden stairs that lead to the kitchen. Some bustling and screams and further struggle precede my aunt making a sudden dive for the stairs, shouting, "Let me get to the girls. I must see the girls."

Further protests are muffled. We do not wait to see what happens next. We bolt back to the sitting-room, slamming the door shut and trying to regain our breath as we press ourselves against it, ready, as we suppose, to protect ourselves against the moment when Auntie Muriel breaks free. We stay there until we hear the van being driven away.

A telegram is sent to my mother who comes back home the next day. Out of our hearing she is told most of the story by Nurse MacKinlay and Granddad although we fill in the bits about the Colgate's toothpowder and the may blossom.

"Poor Muriel," Mother says, "She thought that she was responsible for you while I was away. She has never in her life had to accept responsibility. She has been treated like an invalid all her days. This was all too much for her."

Mother packs a case of Auntie Muriel's clothes and, next day, takes it to the mental hospital. While she is away, a telegram is delivered to say that Gertie, on her return home, had the following morning been found with her head in the gas oven. She is dead. It is signed Jack Hewitt.

Daddy is away from home when all this happens. Mother writes him a letter to put him in the picture. She is harassed at the time and picks up the first scrap of paper that comes to hand.

Daddy is reading the letter and one of his shipmates catches sight of something written on the reverse side of the page.

"Hey, Gerry," he says, "Since when has your wife been telling you what days to change your shirts and your underpants?"

The day we walked the country lanes with Auntie Muriel was the day my grandfather spotted a new housing scheme being built, one of the many inspired by the interest of the Prince of Wales in rehousing people away from the city slums. My mother took little persuading to put her name down for one of the new houses.

"I'm not sure you'll manage on your own, Dad."

"I'll get a daily woman to come in a couple of times a week. I'll come out and see you every Wednesday and Sunday."

"At least that will be two hot meals you'll get. You must bring me your dirty washing."

"Time enough for that. Just think, I'll be able to do the garden for you."

* * *

I think it is June because school hasn't broken up for the summer holidays but it is my last day. It is a Friday and the teacher is reading *King Solomon's Mines* aloud, while we are supposed to be sewing. I'll be glad to leave the sewing behind but sorry that I won't hear what happened to the men that the native people mistook for gods.

A girl in my class is showing me her collection of flower cigarette cards. She says she is only one short of completing the set. She needs the hollyhock. I tell her that I have two at home. She gives me a whole pack of cigarette cards on the understanding that I send her the hollyhock card. I never do send it and for years I carry the guilt.

We have been out to the new house several times to clean. We take the tram to Dovecote shops. It is a very long walk from the tram stop. We walk the full length of Finch Lane and along Colwell Road to reach Southdean Road. We will live in one of the houses in a square leading off Southdean Road. If we were to walk a little further on, we would reach Close's Farm, which is where the housing scheme ends at present as it is not yet completed.

At 95 Southdean Road there are three bedrooms and I am to have one all to myself. I'm delighted because the windowsill is low enough for me to sit on and I'll be like Jo in *Little Women*. In my room there is also a narrow white mantlepiece over an empty grate and I'm thinking about which of my treasures I will display on

118

it. Of course the house is a much smaller than 86 Smith Street. "A lot easier to keep clean," says Mother.

Mother has been packing all her china and saucepans and many other things into tea-chests for weeks. On the day fixed for the removal, the uncles and friends come to carry everything out to the van which has been hired. The two big oak wardrobes and the piano have to be lowered by block and tackle through the upstairs windows. We leave much of the furniture behind because there won't be room for it in the new house and, in any case, we have to leave things cosy for Granddad.

We intend coming back every Saturday to clean at 86 Smith Street.

ISIS publish a wide range of books in large print, from fiction to biography. Any suggestions for books you would like to see in large print or audio are always welcome. Please send to the Editorial department at:

ISIS Publishing Ltd.
7 Centremead
Osney Mead
Oxford OX2 0ES
(01865) 250 333

A full list of titles is available free of charge from:
Ulverscroft large print books

(UK)
The Green
Bradgate Road, Anstey
Leicester LE7 7FU
Tel: (0116) 236 4325

(Australia)
P.O Box 953
Crows Nest
NSW 1585
Tel: (02) 9436 2622

(USA)
1881 Ridge Road
P.O Box 1230, West Seneca,
N.Y. 14224-1230
Tel: (716) 674 4270

(Canada)
P.O Box 80038
Burlington
Ontario L7L 6B1
Tel: (905) 637 8734

(New Zealand)
P.O Box 456
Feilding
Tel: (06) 323 6828

Details of **ISIS** complete and unabridged audio books are also available from these offices. Alternatively, contact your local library for details of their collection of **ISIS** large print and unabridged audio books.